Where's My Mummy?

Also by Maggie Hartley

Where's My Mummy?

LOUISA'S HEART-BREAKING TRUE STORY
OF FAMILY, LOSS AND HOPE

MAGGIE HARTLEY

WITH

HEATHER BISHOP

SEVEN DIALS

First published in Great Britain in 2023 by Seven Dials,
an imprint of The Orion Publishing Group Ltd
Carmelite House, 50 Victoria Embankment
London EC4Y 0DZ

An Hachette UK Company

1 3 5 7 9 10 8 6 4 2

A CIP catalogue record for this book is
available from the British Library.

ISBN (Mass Market Paperback) 978 1 3996 0657 8
ISBN (Audiobook) 978 1 3996 0659 2
ISBN (eBook) 978 1 3996 0658 5

Typeset by Born Group
Printed and bound in Great Britain by Clays Ltd, Elcograf S.p.A.

www.orionbooks.co.uk

Dedication

This book is dedicated to Louisa, my daughter but not through birth. Thank you for your courage, determination, strength and love. I'm so very lucky to have you in my life.

Contents

A Message from Maggie

I wanted to write this book to give people an honest account of what it's like to be a foster carer. To talk about some of the challenges that I face on a day-to-day basis and to talk about some of the children that I've helped.

My main concern throughout all this is to protect the children that have been in my care. For this reason, all names and identifying details have been changed, including my own, and no locations have been included. But I can assure you that all my stories are based on real-life cases told from my own experiences.

Being a foster carer is a privilege and I couldn't imagine doing anything else. My house is never quiet but I wouldn't have it any other way. I hope perhaps that my stories will inspire other people to consider fostering as new carers are always desperately needed.

Maggie Hartley

ONE

As One Door Closes

Taking a swig of my piping hot tea, I shifted around and tried to get comfy on the hard plastic chair.

'Would you like a biscuit?'

A well-spoken woman, with a tiny baby strapped to her in a sling, held out a plate of custard creams and Bourbons.

'Thank you,' I replied, taking one.

She lowered herself down onto the chair next to me.

'I do love a baby group in a church hall,' she sighed. 'You can't beat someone making you a cup of tea that you actually get to drink while it's hot.'

'Oh absolutely,' I smiled, taking another sip from the steaming mug.

I wasn't really in the mood for a long chat with a stranger but I knew she was only being friendly.

'I've come here with all three of my children,' she continued. 'My eldest Wilf is at school now and Monty is due to start nursery in a few weeks.'

She gestured to a curly-haired toddler peddling furiously round the room in a little red and yellow plastic car.

'I'm sure I'll be back here in a few months with this one when she starts crawling around,' she said, glancing down at the baby who was curled up like a hamster against her chest.

'What about you?' she asked. 'How old is your little one?'

I looked down at my feet where eight-month-old Micah was lying on a padded mat on the floor chewing on a plastic giraffe.

Normally I would correct someone and tell them that I was his foster carer, not his mum, as I always think it's a positive thing to talk to people about fostering. There are lots of assumptions about fostering, such as you only foster difficult children, so I think it's good to open people's minds. Children need fostering for all sorts of reasons. Sometimes it's looking after children who have suffered horrific neglect and need to be taken away from their biological parents as they're in danger of being harmed. Or it can be children whose birth parents need a little extra help. Perhaps they are going into hospital and have no one else around to look after their children or they're just not coping with their mental health and need some extra support. I've seen so many different scenarios over the years: I've fostered children whose parents simply can't cope with their disability, refugees who have come to this country completely alone and young parents who need a helping hand to show them how to care for their babies.

Today, however, I knew I probably wouldn't see this woman again and I just didn't have the energy.

'He's eight months, nearly nine, in fact,' I told her, hoping that she wouldn't ask further questions.

'Oh he's tiny,' she gasped. 'Is he not sitting up yet?'

'He was born prematurely,' I explained. 'But he's doing really well and he'll get there in his own time.'

2

'Well, you seem very relaxed about it,' she smiled. 'I wish I was more like you. When Wilf wasn't walking by his first birthday, I was knocking on the GP's door to check there wasn't something wrong.'

I gave her a weak smile.

'Well, I'd better get Monty back for his lunch,' she told me, getting up to go. 'Maybe I'll see you here next week.'

'Perhaps,' I smiled politely.

As I watched her get her things together, I felt a sinking feeling in my stomach. In reality, I knew I wasn't going to be at the baby group next week as tomorrow I was going to be handing Micah over to his new adoptive parents.

I always felt such a mixture of emotions when a child left.

I was so happy that he'd found his forever home. The couple, Dionne and Jamie, seemed lovely and I had liked them instantly. They already had a ten-year-old son but they'd struggled to conceive again for years and had gone through multiple rounds of IVF without success.

They were the perfect match; in fact, it almost seemed meant to be. Micah's birth mother's family was from Jamaica – just like Dionne's family – so they had that cultural connection.

I reached down and lifted Micah up off the floor. He gave me a big grin as I sat him on my knee.

'You're such a sweetheart, aren't you?' I told him, planting a kiss on his soft cheek.

I knew I was going to miss him terribly. This smiley little boy with a strong spirit had stolen my heart. Micah had come straight into the care system at birth. His biological mum was in her late teens and had already had two older children who had both been taken into care at birth.

Social Services had tried to offer her support throughout her third pregnancy in the hope that she could perhaps keep this baby but she'd gone off the radar. She hadn't gone to any midwife appointments or scans and she hadn't turned up for meetings with Social Services. There was a suspicion that she'd been drinking throughout her pregnancy and Micah was born five weeks early, weighing just under 2lb. He'd spent the first six weeks of his life in the NICU (newborn intensive care unit) before coming to me. Nobody knew what the impact of his mother's lifestyle would have on him until he grew older but there was a strong possibility that he would have Fetal Alcohol Syndrome, although it was hard to diagnose until he got older and any developmental delays became more apparent.

He hadn't been an easy baby by any means. He woke several times a night for a bottle and didn't nap much during the day. If his milk wasn't at exactly the right temperature, he'd shake his head and push it away and, so far, he wasn't really that keen on food. He was a determined little thing with a strong will and I'd completely fallen in love with him. He gave the best cuddles and his smile could melt even the hardest person's heart.

Even though I'd said goodbye to many children over the years, I'd found the last few days hard. I loved babies and I couldn't help but get attached to them. You cared for them 24/7 for weeks or months and they got very attached to you too. It's a very intense experience and your days are full with looking after them and I got such joy in seeing them develop and reach their first milestones. Then when they leave, I feel such a sense of loss and emptiness. It was difficult knowing

4

that was coming and I had to say goodbye. There had been a few tears as I'd washed all of Micah's clothes and packed his things up for his new home. I never normally went to playgroups but today I felt like I needed to get out of the house and try to escape from my own thoughts for a little while.

The playgroup was run by two grey-haired older women from the church who I could tell doted on the babies.

'Lovely to see you, Mum,' one of them said to me as I pulled Micah's coat on getting ready to leave.

'We're going to be doing some singing next week,' she added. 'I bet your little one would enjoy that.'

'Oh lovely,' I smiled, not having the heart to tell her that next week Micah would be with his new parents.

I took him home for lunch and afterwards, I put him down for a nap. Normally he'd fight sleep and most days he made such a fuss that I'd end up getting him out of his cot in the end. However, today he curled up straight away and closed his eyes. Perhaps the playgroup had worn him out or he sensed that big changes were happening?

It gave me the opportunity to pack the last of Micah's things.

No one knew how long it would take for the right family to be matched with him so I'd already bought lots of nine to twelve-month-old clothes that were still huge for him. I was going to send them to Jamie and Dionne's with the rest of his stuff.

I was just sorting through a pile of Babygros when my mobile rang.

'How are you doing, Maggie?' asked a cheery voice.

It was my supervising social worker, Anna, calling from Social Services. We hadn't worked together for long but I liked her. She was newly qualified and had all the optimism and energy of someone just starting out in their career. She was always very positive, which made a nice change from some of the older, more jaded social workers who had been at Social Services for years. It was an extremely hard job and it always seemed to take its toll in the end.

'How were Dionne and Jamie last night? she asked. 'Did it go well?'

Ever since a panel had approved the match two weeks ago, they had been coming over and spending time with Micah. Yesterday they had taken him out for the day and then stayed for tea after coming back with him, along with their son Taylor.

'It went really well,' I told her. 'They're so easy to get along with and Taylor's a really lovely boy.'

'That's great news,' Anna replied. 'Nita emailed me earlier to say we're all on track for tomorrow.'

Nita was Micah's social worker.

'Yep, they're coming to collect him in the morning,' I told her. 'In fact, I'm just getting the last of his things together.'

It was definitely one of the hardest parts of my job – the letting go. Particularly when it was a baby who didn't understand what was happening. Even though I had never referred to myself as Micah's mum, I was the first person that he saw every morning when he opened his eyes and the last person he saw when he went to sleep at night. I was the one who had fed him his bottles and paced up and down with him for hours on end when he wasn't feeling well. For nearly eight months, I had been the one constant in his life but from tomorrow, I wouldn't be there any more.

6

I could see that he liked Dionne and Jamie and they were brilliant with him. But when they had brought him back last night he had immediately reached his arms out to me.

'He'll be fine,' Anna reassured me, as soon as he came in the door.

'Oh, I know he will be,' I sighed.

I knew instinctively that Micah had found his forever home and he would quickly grow to love his new family. It didn't mean that it hurt any less though.

For the eight months that I'd had Micah, other children had come and gone but he was the only one living with me now. As he was only a baby, there was no point in having a party or a big farewell for him. The best thing for me to do on his final day was to keep things stable and consistent.

After Micah woke up from his nap, we had a quiet afternoon. The plan was that Dionne and Jamie would come round first thing in the morning. I knew they were desperate to get him home and settled and there was no point in prolonging the goodbye for me.

Dionne called later that afternoon to see how Micah was doing.

I could hear the excitement fizzing in her voice.

'His room's all ready,' she told me. 'Taylor's so excited. I don't think he's going to sleep tonight.'

'What time do you want us to collect him in the morning?' she asked me.

'If you come at 9.30 a.m. I'll make sure that he's packed and ready to go,' I told her.

Even though I was trying to keep things normal for Micah, I lingered over every moment of his bedtime that night. I let him splash around in the bath for ages. As I gave him a bottle,

I relished every second of feeling his small but strong little body in my arms. I took in all the details so I'd remember them – the way he always had one little hand on his bottle, his eyes fluttering as he got more sleepy. He'd never done it before but tonight he fell asleep in my arms and I let him stay there until my arm went numb. I kissed the top of his head and gently lowered him into his cot. He murmured slightly then rolled onto his side.

'Night night, little man,' I whispered. 'You've got a big day tomorrow.'

Then I went downstairs and busied myself with more sorting and packing until it was time for me to go to bed too.

By the time I heard Micah stirring just after 6 a.m. the following morning, I felt like I had hardly slept. But there was still lots to do before Dionne and Jamie arrived.

When the doorbell went just before 9.30 a.m., I had just washed the last of Micah's bottles and packed them all into a bag.

As I opened the door, Dionne handed me a huge bunch of flowers.

'Oh how lovely,' I smiled.

'We just wanted to say thank you for looking after our son,' she told me. 'We already love him so much and we're so grateful to you for everything.'

Her voice cracked with emotion.

'Sorry,' she sniffled. 'I told myself I wouldn't get emotional this morning but I can't help it. I'm a wreck!'

'We've been waiting a long time for this,' Jamie told me.

'And so has Micah,' I smiled. 'He's all ready to go.'

While I helped Jamie load up the car with his things, Dionne sat on the floor and played with Micah.

Then came the moment that I had been dreading.

'It's time to go now bubba,' Dionne cooed as she strapped him into his car seat.

I did my best to hold it together as I kissed the top of his head and stroked his cheek.

'Bye-bye little man,' I told him. 'I know you're going to have the best life with your new mummy and daddy.'

Dionne was crying as she gave me a hug.

'Thank you so much for everything,' she said.

'Go and enjoy your son,' I told her. 'Keep in touch and let me know if you need anything.'

'Yes and you must come and visit us,' Jamie told me.

I'd love nothing more but with a baby Micah's age, I knew that I needed to let go completely. At least until several months had passed and he was a lot older. He needed that time to settle and get attached to his new parents and I knew that seeing me too soon would only confuse that.

'I hope you understand but I won't come out to the car with you,' I told them. 'I don't think big emotional goodbyes are good for anyone.'

'Of course,' smiled Jamie.

I wanted to keep it very low key for Micah's sake and I didn't want to risk him getting upset. I watched from the window as they drove away and, as their car disappeared off down the street and into the distance, I finally allowed myself to have a little cry.

'Onwards and upwards, Maggie,' I told myself.

Then I threw myself into my therapy – cleaning and sorting. There wasn't an inch of my house that didn't get vacuumed or scrubbed that afternoon. Sheets were changed, surfaces were wiped and I did all the little niggly jobs that I had been putting off for months.

By late afternoon, I was absolutely exhausted. I'd just stopped to make myself a cup of coffee when the phone rang.

It was Anna.

'How did it go?' she asked.

'Really well,' I told her. 'They were so happy.'

'Well it sounds like he's settling in really well,' she replied. 'I spoke to Nita earlier and she said she had called them and they were giving Micah a bath.'

'Aw that's lovely,' I smiled.

I was genuinely delighted for them. People adopted for all sorts of reasons. Sometimes they had fertility problems like Dionne and Jamie, but that wasn't always the case. Some people had a burning desire to adopt. It could be that they were adopted as a child and wanted to give something back, or perhaps they were a gay couple or a single parent and adoption was their preferred way to start their own family.

'And how are you doing?' Anna asked.

'Oh you know,' I sighed. 'It's always sad when a child leaves. I'm only human. Especially babies as you can't help but get so attached to them. But that's the nature of my job; I went into fostering to help as many children as I can.'

'Actually that's what I wanted to talk to you about,' Anna told me. 'Could I pop round tomorrow and have a chat to you about something?'

There was suddenly a serious tone to her voice.

'Of course,' I said. 'What's happened? Should I be worried?'

'Oh no, not at all,' she said. 'One of my colleagues was talking to me about a possible placement and your name came up. And obviously the timing's good with Micah leaving. It's a child who needs quite specialist care. I didn't want to bother you with it now as I know today has been tough for you.'

'OK,' I said. 'Tomorrow will be fine.'

We arranged for her to pop in for a coffee the following morning.

That night, after all the emotion and the activity of the day, I was in bed by 9.30 p.m. When I woke up at 8.30 a.m the next morning I felt like a new woman. I hadn't slept for that long in months.

There was just enough time for me to have a quick shower and get some breakfast before Anna arrived.

'Let me give you a hug,' she said as she walked through the door. 'Yesterday must have been hard for you as I know how much you cared for Micah.'

'You know me. I love my babies,' I smiled.

'I've said this to you before, but I honestly don't know how you do it,' she said.

Saying goodbye was never easy but I knew it was something that I had to do. Helping a child to move on was my job and I had to focus on the positives. Micah was a happy, healthy little boy who had found his forever home. He was going to live with two parents who loved him and I was sure he was going to grow up in a happy, stable environment. That was everything I wanted for him and I had to put my own feelings of loss to one side.

We chit-chatted as I made us both a coffee.

'So,' I said as I sat down at the kitchen table with her. 'What's this placement that you wanted to talk to me about?'

Anna took a sip of coffee before she started to explain.

'I don't think I've ever come across a situation quite like this before,' she told me. 'It's a really tragic case and quite upsetting, which is why I wanted to talk to you about it face to face.'

My heart sank and my mind immediately thought of neglect. I'd fostered children who had been victims of severe neglect before and it was always unbearable to see little ones who had suffered so much.

'We're potentially looking for someone to foster a thirteen-year-old girl,' she told me.

'Potentially?' I asked. 'Has she been taken into care yet?'

'Well, this is the thing,' explained Anna. 'She's actually in hospital in a coma at the moment.'

Shocked and intrigued, I listened as she explained how the girl, who was called Louisa, and her parents, had been in a head-on car crash four days ago.

'The police are still investigating what happened but it looks like they lost control on a sharp bend of a country lane and hit a tree. The parents both died on impact. Louisa, who was in the back seat, was the only survivor. She's badly injured but for now she's alive.'

'That's horrific,' I sighed, shaking my head. 'Poor girl.'

Anna described how she had some swelling on the brain and injuries to her legs.

'But despite all of that, the doctors are hopeful that she could wake up and make a full recovery,' she told me.

I just couldn't get my head around it. Two parents dead and a child in a coma. In a few minutes her whole family had been totally destroyed. Even if she did survive, how on earth would she ever get over something like that?

TWO

A Life Shattered

It was one of the saddest things that I'd ever heard. I couldn't stop thinking about this poor girl lying in hospital in a coma.

'What were her parents' names?' I asked Anna.

'Karen and Simon,' she replied. 'From what we've found out so far, Louisa was an only child and they'd had her later in life. They were both in their mid-fifties.'

'Are there no other relatives around who could take her?' I asked.

'Investigations are ongoing but from what the police have found out so far, it doesn't look like it. They've been struggling to find a next of kin.'

Karen's mother was in her eighties and in a local nursing home.

'She has dementia sadly so she doesn't have the mental capacity to even understand what has happened,' sighed Anna.

The police had managed to trace Simon's brother in Australia.

'He was very shocked apparently but I don't think he and Simon were close,' she continued. 'He hadn't seen him in over fifteen years and he's never met Louisa. So, bearing all that in mind, we need to start looking for other options. There might be family friends around but no one has come forward yet.'

A children's home would normally be another option for a child of Louisa's age but she would need specialist care and it made sense that, after everything this young girl had been through, a foster home would be the best place for her.

'So I wondered if you would consider taking her, Maggie?' Anna asked. 'It would be an intense placement. If she pulls through, she's going to need a lot of support, both physical and emotional. We appreciate that it's a big undertaking – that's why I wanted to run it by you.'

'I know it sounds harsh but do we even know if she's going to survive?' I asked.

Anna explained that the doctors were hopeful that Louisa would pull through. Her motor responses were good and she had made some eye movements.

'They're all good signs apparently,' she told me. 'There are no guarantees but they feel the odds are in her favour. Assuming she does wake up, no one knows when that's going to be – we really do need to get a plan in place so, if and when Louisa does come out of the coma, we can communicate to her what's going to happen.'

There was so much to take in and think about.

'I know it's a lot, especially when Micah's just left,' Anna added. 'We don't need an immediate answer but we're hoping to have a professionals' meeting in the next couple of days so ideally we want to have a foster carer on board by then.'

'Of course,' I said. 'That's understandable.'

Poor kid. Even if she did wake up, everything around her had gone. Her parents were dead. She had literally lost everything.

14

'What if I don't think I can manage the medical side of things?' I asked. 'As you know, I'm a single carer so there's no one else around to help me lift or bathe her.'

I'd been relatively young when I'd got into fostering. I'd always worked with children and seemed to have a natural affinity with them, especially kids who were deemed to be challenging. When I left school, I got a job in a residential children's home, then worked for Social Services as a family support assistant and then as a deputy matron at a residential boarding school for maladjusted boys. I knew I wanted to work with children but after four years, I left and became a childminder. By the time I was twenty-seven, I fancied a new challenge and that's when I thought about fostering. For some strange reason, I liked stroppy kids and they seemed to respond well to me. It didn't seem to bother Social Services that I was single and I was approved to take up to three placements. Since then, I'd never looked back. All sorts of placements had followed, from newborn babies like Micah right up to teenagers and even young adults.

Fostering wasn't just a job, it was a vocation, and with so many children coming and going over the years, my personal life had taken a back seat. I'd had boyfriends occasionally but so far, no one who was special enough for me to want to share my life and my fostering with. I didn't mind; I had a good circle of loyal friends around me who would always help out when they could. That included some fellow foster carers who just 'got it' and were always there for advice and support.

Anna nodded.

'It's hard to know what her medical needs are going to be but rest assured we won't leave you to cope alone. We'll put a proper care plan in place and make sure that there's lots of help and support available.'

She explained that I would have contact with an occupational therapy team and there was a disability team social worker who could cover a few hours a week if I needed to go out anywhere or do shopping.

I had other concerns too. I had the space to take on three foster children at any one time but a demanding placement like this meant I wouldn't have the capacity to foster anyone else.

Fostering had always been more than just a job to me, it was a vocation. But it also paid my bills and I couldn't afford not to have any income for months while Louisa was in a coma and then just have the one placement.

'You know I don't do what I do for money,' I explained to Anna. 'No one is ever going to get rich from fostering. But I've still got a mortgage to pay and I can't see how it would work for me financially as Louisa would have to be a solo placement and I wouldn't be able to foster any other children.'

'I completely understand,' she replied. 'We'd make sure that we were paying you an enhanced fee so it would be the equivalent of fostering two children. And as Louisa hopefully recovers, she will be able to claim disability allowance and you would be eligible to claim carer's allowance as well.'

But I had to think of the practicalities and there was also the fact that no one knew if and when she would wake up from her coma. I couldn't be without an income indefinitely while she was in hospital.

It was as if Anna could tell what I was thinking.

'I appreciate that we'd need you to keep the placement open for her while she's in hospital so we'd pay you a solo placement fee until Louisa was discharged and came to live with you. I know we need to make this financially viable for you, Maggie, and if you decide to go ahead, I'll make sure it gets signed off before the professionals' meeting.'

'Thank you,' I said. 'I really appreciate that.'

Despite all the reassurances, I still needed time to think about it.

'I know it's a lot to take in but let me know when you've made a decision,' Anna told me.

After she finished her coffee, she had to get back to the office.

'Where were they going?' I asked as I walked her to the front door.

'What do you mean? she asked.

'Louisa and her parents. Where were they driving to or from?'

'Oh, the police said they had just been to pick up their new puppy from the breeder.'

I imagined this little family and how happy and excited they must have been in the car home.

'Did the puppy survive the crash?' I asked.

Anna shook her head sadly.

'Have a think, Maggie, and let me know,' she told me as she walked down the front path.

It was all I thought about for the rest of the day, about this poor girl lying in hospital, unaware that her parents and her life as she knew it had been completely obliterated. It was just so sad.

But was I really the right person for the job? Could I help this child through both her grief and her recovery?

That night I called my friend and fellow foster carer Vicky. I knew I could speak to her in confidence about it.

'Oh Maggie, that's awful,' she gasped when I told her about it. 'How tragic. I think I might have read about the crash in the paper the other day.'

'If she pulls through, she's going to need a lot of care,' I sighed. 'Do you think I can do that on my own?'

'Of course you can,' Vicky told me. 'She's going to need a lot of love, kindness and patience and you have that in spades. She'd be lucky to have you.'

'I wish I had as much confidence in myself as you have in me,' I laughed.

'Maggie, you know that you're not going to say no to her so I don't even know why you're debating it,' Vicky told me.

She was right. I could never turn my back on a child who so desperately needed a safety net.

I called Anna the following morning.

'I've thought long and hard about it and I'm willing to foster Louisa,' I told her.

'That's brilliant,' she replied. 'I'm so, so pleased.'

The first thing I needed to do was attend a professionals' meeting at Social Services in a couple of days' time. It was going to be useful as it would give me a lot more information about Louisa, her life and how things might work going forwards, although I realised that a lot of it was still unknown as things stood.

On the morning of the meeting, Anna was there to greet me.

'This is my colleague, Brian,' she told me, introducing me to a slightly balding man in his fifties wearing a striped polo shirt tucked into his jeans. 'He's been appointed as Louisa's social worker.'

'Hello Margaret,' he said, shaking my hand vigorously.

'It's Maggie actually,' I smiled. 'Margaret sounds very formal.'

'Oh I'm sorry,' he said.

Brian's team manager, Sharon, was leading the meeting and she went round the table introducing everyone.

'This is DC Lee Jenkins,' she said, gesturing to a red-haired man in his thirties in a suit.

'Hi all,' he nodded.

There was also a teacher from Louisa's secondary school who introduced herself as Tammy Grey. She was also head of Year Eight.

'Brian is Louisa's social worker and Maggie is a foster carer who, all being well, is going to be fostering Louisa when she's discharged from hospital.'

She handed over to DC Jenkins first to update us all on the situation.

'I'm sure as you all already know, sadly as a result of a Road Traffic Accident, both Karen and Simon Baker were killed on impact. Their thirteen-year-old daughter Louisa remains in a coma in hospital.'

He described how there would eventually be an inquest into the crash and a file had been passed to the coroner.

'It's just speculation at the moment, but initially it looks like Mr Baker lost control on a tight bend. We're waiting for toxicology tests to come back but we don't expect there to be any evidence of drink or drugs and there were no other vehicles involved.'

He described how one possible theory they were looking at was that Mr Baker had been distracted in some way by the new puppy.

'Everything points to it being a tragic accident,' he said.

He explained how the police had been trying to trace Louisa's next of kin, after her parents.

'As Karen's mother, Irene, isn't mentally fit, the next of kin is Simon's brother, Martin Baker, who lives in Australia. He hadn't seen his brother for fifteen years but had spoken to him occasionally.

'Mr Baker is doing as much as he can from Melbourne. The bodies have been released to a funeral director and he's registered their deaths. He feels it's best to wait at least a few weeks to organise a funeral, until we know more about Louisa's condition.'

The thought made me shudder that she could wake up from a coma to find out that not only had her parents died but that they had also been laid to rest so she couldn't say goodbye.

'Where are we at in terms of the family home?' asked Sharon.

DC Jenkins described how the family had rented the same three-bedroom terrace house for the past five years. The plumbing company that Simon Baker had worked for for the past decade had kindly agreed to cover the rent for the next few months.

'That will give everyone time until things are more sorted and we know what's happening with Louisa,' he added.

It was all such a sad state of affairs.

Sharon then introduced everyone to Miss Grey, who looked visibly upset.

'I just want to say that the whole school is devastated about what's happened to Louisa and her family,' she sighed, looking close to tears. 'I didn't know Mr and Mrs Baker well, but Louisa is a lovely girl. She's very kind and helpful.

She's been her tutor group rep for the past year as she's very responsible. I know her friends are upset about what's happened to her and they want her to know that we're all thinking about her.'

Brian explained they had been hoping someone from the hospital could attend the meeting but understandably they were too busy.

'Having spoken to her consultant myself this morning, Louisa is showing some really positive signs of recovery,' he said. 'Obviously things can change very quickly but at present she's stable and we have everything crossed that she will eventually come out of this.'

He also explained that at this stage it was impossible to know exactly how much rehab she would need.

'But what they did say was that her injuries are all recoverable. The swelling on her brain is reducing without her needing surgery and she's got a broken leg. It's just a case of wait and see.'

Brian then talked that about what would happen if and when Louisa recovered enough to leave hospital.

'In the meantime we do need to come up with a plan about where Louisa can go,' he said. 'Unfortunately her uncle in Australia doesn't feel that he's in a position to offer Louisa full-time care – he's single and travels a lot for work and he's never met his niece. He feels it would be in her best interests to remain in the UK where she's settled in school.

'So we are very thankful that Maggie has stepped in,' he continued. 'She's an experienced carer who is happy to take Louisa on as a solo placement.'

'I'd like to start visiting Louisa as soon as I can,' I told him.

'I'm sure we can clear that with the hospital,' Sharon nodded.

I was a stranger to Louisa but I hated the thought of no one being by her bedside.

I'd seen films and TV programmes where people had woken up from comas and said they had been able to hear their loved ones or nurses talking to them.

'I think that's a good idea,' nodded Anna.

'I'm sure we can clear it with the ICU,' added Brian.

I turned to Miss Grey.

'Do you think it would be possible for me to have a chat to some of Louisa's friends?' I asked. 'I'd love to know more about her.'

I wanted to try to build up a picture of who she was, the things she liked doing and any music or books that she enjoyed.

'Yes of course,' said Miss Grey. 'I'll check with the head but I'm sure we can arrange that.'

Brian told me that they would get a placement agreement organised as soon as possible. That would give me delegated responsibility, which meant hospital staff could talk to me about Louisa's condition and any treatment that she needed. I couldn't consent to any surgeries but it meant they could keep me updated.

'Would it be possible for me to go into the family home at all?' I asked. 'I'd love to be able to take Louisa some of her things to have around her in the hospital?'

'I'm sure we can arrange that,' said Brian.

DC Jenkins nodded.

'We have the keys at the moment. We obtained access to the house and changed the locks so we can sort something out.'

Like me, everyone had been moved by this young girl's plight and we were all willing to pull together and do whatever we could to help her.

I came out of the meeting feeling like I'd made progress and I was one step closer to getting to know Louisa. The next thing I needed to do was to go and visit her in hospital and, to be honest, I was absolutely dreading it.

THREE

Building Up a Picture

My hand lingered over the buzzer on the door that said Intensive Care Unit. I took a deep breath and pressed it, ignoring the flutter of nerves I felt in my stomach.

I didn't really know why I was nervous. I think it was more a fear of the unknown. I'd never seen anyone in a coma before and I didn't quite know what to expect.

I'd never met Louisa but already I felt a real sense of responsibility for her. At this moment in time, she had no one else to care for her except me.

There was no sign of anyone coming to the door so I pressed the buzzer again and waited. Eventually a nurse came to let me in.

'I'm here to see Louisa Baker,' I told her. 'My name's Maggie Hartley.'

I explained that I was a foster carer and she nodded in a way that suggested she was aware of the situation.

'Poor lass,' she sighed. 'She's been through the mill but she's hanging on in there and she's doing well.'

She led me down the corridor to a nurses' station in the middle of the ward where a red-haired woman in her forties was sat at a computer.

'This is Claire, our senior charge nurse,' she told me.

The nurse explained who I was to her.

'Hopefully Social Services have cleared it with you but I'll be coming to visit Louisa most days,' I told her. 'It would be really helpful if you could update me about how she's doing and if anything has happened overnight. I'll also leave you my phone number in case you ever need to get hold of me urgently.'

'That's great,' she replied. 'I had a call from someone at Social Services letting me know that you'd be coming and we've put you down as the main contact.'

'Thank you,' I nodded.

'If you go with Wendy, she'll take you through to see Louisa now.'

I followed the other nurse down a short corridor until we got to a room at the end. It was so quiet except for the beeps of a variety of machines.

'It can be a bit alarming at first but I'll talk you through everything once we get in there,' Wendy told me kindly.

'Hello Louisa,' she said cheerfully as we walked into the room. 'You've got a visitor here to see you.'

I swallowed a lump in my throat as my eyes took in the figure lying in the bed. She was so battered and bruised. Her head was bandaged and even though her eyes were closed, I could see they were both swollen and black. There were deep lacerations to her face and I could see that one of her legs was in a cast.

'Oh my goodness,' I gasped. 'The poor girl.'

There didn't seem to be one single part of her that wasn't black and blue.

'She's lucky to be alive,' sighed Wendy. 'The police said the car was a wreck. She's been through it but she's a real fighter, aren't you, Louisa?' she said loudly, giving her arm an affectionate stroke.

Wendy got me a seat by Louisa's bed and talked me through all of the tubes and wires that were coming out of various parts of Louisa's body – the feeding tube in her nose and the IV in her arm for fluids that were keeping her alive, the reassuring but constant bleep of the machines that were monitoring her blood pressure and breathing. The lights in the room were down low and it was almost futuristic. I'd never seen anyone as badly injured and it was overwhelming.

Wendy must have seen the worried look on my face.

'I know it's a lot to take in but it's a lot less scary once you know what they all do,' she told me.

'Do you think that she will wake up soon?' I asked her. 'Can she really recover from all of this?'

Wendy shrugged.

'I wish I could tell you for certain but as far as comas go, it's impossible to predict,' she sighed. 'But she's young and strong and so far, all of the signs are good.'

She explained that she was breathing on her own and the swelling on her brain was slowly going down.

'It's only been a few days and she's improved a lot already,' she told me. 'She's a little fighter.'

She gently patted the top of Louisa's hand.

'I'm going to leave you with Maggie now, darling,' Wendy said loudly. 'She's going to be keeping you company.'

'It's nice the way you talk to her,' I told her.

'Oh I like to chat to all of my patients,' Wendy smiled. 'I know they're in a coma but I'm convinced that somewhere, deep down in their subconscious, they can hear us.'

She described how every day they washed Louisa and moved her so she didn't get pressure sores. Physiotherapists came in and pummelled her chest to stop a build-up of fluid in her lungs. There was a whole team of people whose job it was to keep her alive.

'Research has shown that it's good to stimulate coma patients in any way that you can,' Wendy told me. 'Whether that's through touch, sound or smell, so I always talk away to them.'

'I've read that too,' I nodded.

'She even has to put up with my singing, poor love,' she laughed. 'Right I've got to get on but I'll leave you two to have a chat.'

'Thank you,' I said.

I pulled my chair up closer to Louisa's bed and reached for her hand. It felt soft and warm.

Even though I was a stranger to her, I wanted to reassure her that she wasn't alone and there was someone there.

I cleared my throat.

'Hi Louisa,' I told her. 'You don't know me but my name's Maggie and I'm a foster carer.'

It felt so strange talking out loud to someone who couldn't respond and I didn't even know if she could hear me. I didn't want to say too much in case she could hear me and was wondering where her parents were and why on earth I was there.

'There are so many people thinking about you and everyone wants you to get better.'

I squeezed her hand.

Suddenly I noticed her eyes fluttering and her arm twitched.

I shot up from my chair and ran to the door.

'I need help!' I shouted, panicked. 'Can someone please help me?'

A nurse popped her head out of one of the rooms and ran down the corridor towards me.

'I was holding her hand and talking to her and suddenly she started moving,' I explained. 'Her eyes were fluttering and I'm sure that her arm moved.'

But when I turned and looked at the bed, Louisa was still again.

The nurse went over to the monitors and checked everything.

'Is she OK?' I asked. 'Do you think she could be waking up?'

'Everything looks fine,' the nurse reassured me. 'Her vitals are all stable.'

'Why was she moving then?' I asked.

'Sometimes people in comas make involuntary movements,' she told me. 'I know it can look frightening but it's nothing to worry about.'

It had really given me a fright – I had so much to learn.

Even though I didn't know Louisa, I wanted her to know that people did care about her. Her room looked so stark – there were no cards or flowers by her bed or any personal items at all.

'It's very bare in here but don't worry, I'm going to make it nice and cosy for you,' I told her.

I stayed for another half an hour.

'I'm going to go now,' I told Louisa. 'But I'll be back later.'

I had an appointment at Louisa's secondary school and it was a forty-five-minute drive from the hospital. It was a huge Sixties' building with a modern extension on the side. It was lunchtime when I got there so it was incredibly noisy and the playground was packed.

I signed in at reception and Miss Grey came out to meet me.

'Hi Maggie,' she smiled. 'How are things?'

I told her that I'd been to the hospital to visit Louisa.

'Oh, how was she?' she asked.

I described how she looked very badly injured but the staff seemed nice and were very positive.

'There are no guarantees but all the signs are good and she's hanging on in there.'

'I really hope so,' she replied. 'We've all been thinking of her.'

She told me how Louisa's tutor group had made a card for her and how all her classmates had signed it.

'That's lovely, I'll take that up to the hospital with me later,' I said. 'Her room looks so bare so it will help to brighten things up.'

Three of Louisa's friends had agreed to have a chat with me and Miss Grey led me to an office where they were waiting. They looked really nervous.

'Girls, this is Maggie,' Miss Grey told them. 'Maggie's a foster carer and hopefully when Louisa gets better and leaves the hospital, Louisa will go and live with her.'

The girls stared at me and gave me weak smiles.

'Maggie, this is Becky, Phoenix and Frankie. They are Louisa's closest friends.'

'Thank you for agreeing to chat to me,' I told them. 'I went to see Louisa at the hospital this morning and I'd love to take her a few things for her room and I wondered if you would be able to tell me the kind of things that she liked.'

'What does she look like?' Becky asked.

'Is she definitely going to get better?' Phoenix added.

Frankie, a small blonde girl, didn't say a word.

'She looks very peaceful and settled, just as if she's in a very deep sleep,' I told them. 'Unfortunately she was very badly injured and nobody knows for sure what's going to happen. But the nurses say she's doing well and everyone is very hopeful that once her brain recovers, she will wake up.'

'I know it's hard, girls,' Miss Grey told them. 'But we'll just have to wait and see.'

They nodded sadly. I didn't want to give them false hope and I wanted to be honest.

'It would be great if you could tell me some of the things that Louisa liked doing,' I explained. 'Sometimes when people are in a coma it's good to play them music that they like or read them their favourite books. Hearing familiar voices is also good so if you wanted to, you could even record a message for Louisa and I can play it to her.'

They nodded.

'What kind of things does she like to do?' I asked them. I was trying to build up a picture of her in my mind.

'Gymnastics,' said Phoenix.

'Yeah she's really good,' added Becky. 'She's been doing it since she was little and she's won loads of competitions and got medals.'

'She really likes babies and animals too and she wants to be a vet nurse when she leaves school,' added Phoenix. 'She couldn't wait to get their new puppy, Luna. She was so excited.'

At the mention of the puppy, they all looked really upset.

'Miss Grey said Luna died too,' sighed Phoenix.

'I know and I'm so sorry,' I said.

We chatted a little bit more about Louisa and the things that she liked.

'What sort of music was she into?' I asked them.

'Mainly chart stuff,' shrugged Becky. 'They always had Radio 1 on in the car and in the kitchen at home.'

'And this might sound like a strange question but were there any smells that she liked? Did she use any perfumes or body sprays or were there any toiletries that she particularly liked?'

'She really loved her mum's perfume,' Phoenix told me. 'The really fancy Chanel one.'

'Yeah, her dad bought it for her mum every Christmas and she went mad as it was really expensive and Louisa was always going into her bedroom and spraying herself with it' smiled Becky.

At the mention of Karen, they all suddenly looked close to tears.

'I'm so sorry about Louisa's mum,' I told them. 'She sounds like a lovely lady.'

They nodded.

'It's just so sad,' sighed Becky.

'She was really nice,' added Phoenix. 'She was always really kind. She was a hairdresser so when Louisa had a gymnastics competition she would do her hair for her in a bun. And sometimes if we went for a sleepover then she'd do our hair in these really cool French braids.'

'Her dad was nice too,' Becky said. 'They were really excited about getting Luna. We were going to go round and see her, and Louisa wanted her to sleep in her room. She was so happy.'

'What do you think, Frankie?' Miss Grey asked. 'Is there anything that you'd like to pass on to Maggie about Louisa?'

While the rest of us had been chatting, she hadn't said a single word.

Suddenly she burst into tears.

'Oh Frankie,' sighed Miss Grey. 'Are you OK?'

She went over and put her an arm around Frankie.

The poor girl was crying so hard, she could hardly get her words out.

'Is Louisa going to die?' she snivelled. 'I don't want her to die.'

'The doctors are doing all they can to make sure that she's comfortable,' I told her. 'Nobody knows for sure but they're hopeful that she can make a full recovery.'

I felt awful for upsetting her but I didn't want to give anyone false hope. The sad fact was that no one knew if Louisa was going to pull through. She'd been in a horrific car crash and when it came to brain injuries, there were no guarantees.

As Phoenix and Becky comforted Frankie, Miss Grey came over to me.

'I think it would be a good idea to wrap things up now,' she told me in a low voice.

I nodded in agreement.

'Thank you so much, girls, for being so helpful,' I told them. 'Louisa's very lucky to have such good friends. I'll tell Louisa that you're all thinking about her and I'll keep Miss Grey updated about how she is.'

'Can we see her?' Frankie asked, wiping her nose. 'Could we come to the hospital and visit her?'

'Well, what I can do is give Miss Grey my phone number and she can pass it on to your parents. They are very welcome to ring me and we can try to arrange something with the hospital if they're in agreement.'

They all nodded.

'Thank you,' said Phoenix.

Miss Grey walked me back to reception.

'Thanks for arranging that,' I told Miss Grey. 'I really feel for them. I can see how upset they are.'

'Not a problem,' she said. 'I hope it helps in some small way. As I said in the meeting the other day, everyone is devastated by what's happened. We're all really worried about her so please do keep us updated.'

'I promise I will,' I said.

I gave her my phone number and took the card that Louisa's tutor group had made, which was covered with lovely messages.

'I'll make sure that I read all of those out to her,' I told her.

Before I left, there was one more thing that I wanted to ask.

'What's Louisa like?' I asked Miss Grey.

'She is honestly the sweetest, most kind-hearted person,' she told me. 'She's always so polite and well-behaved but more importantly, she really looks after people and stands up for them.'

'That's nice to hear,' I smiled. 'She sounds like a genuinely lovely girl.'

'She really is,' sighed Miss Grey. 'We just hope to have her back at school soon.'

I wanted to go back to the hospital that evening so I went home to quickly grab some lunch then drove to the local retail park.

I wanted Louisa to feel cared for and looked after. I went to Boots and bought her a washbag and then got some essentials such as a toothbrush, a flannel, some lip balm and some nice body wash. Then I went to the perfume counter and bought a small bottle of Chanel No5. I thought even a little bit sprayed on her pillow might help stimulate her memory. I also popped into a card shop and got her a little Jellycat rabbit that I knew even a teenager would find cute. I knew fresh flowers weren't allowed in the ICU because of the risk of infection so I picked up some fake sunflowers and a little vase in the supermarket just to help brighten up her hospital room.

It was late afternoon before I got back to the hospital.

'Someone's been busy,' smiled Wendy as she saw me walking down the ward with two carrier bags.

'I wanted to make the room feel a little bit cosier for her,' I replied.

This time, I felt as if I knew a little bit more about Louisa and I had lots I could chat to her about.

'I saw Phoenix, Becky and Frankie today,' I told her as I arranged the sunflowers in the vase and put them on top of the cupboard next to her bed. 'They're all missing you and they want you to get well. And Miss Grey sent her love too,' I added.

I put the little Jellycat rabbit next to the sunflowers then I put her new toiletries in the cupboard and sprayed a tiny bit of the Chanel perfume onto her pillow.

'Ooh it smells lovely in here,' said a nurse, coming in to check on her vitals.

'Is it OK to spray things?' I asked, worried.

'Yes of course,' she said. 'Anything sensory is good for coma patients. You can put objects in their hands or play music for them if you want.'

'Could I bring a radio up the next time I come?' I asked.

'Yes of course,' she said. 'We don't recommend anything too loud or to play it for too long, but it's definitely worth doing.'

'We've had patients who come out of comas and they swear that they remember songs or music that were played to them when they were unconscious,' she told me. 'The brain works in mysterious ways.'

Then I sat at Louisa's bedside and read all of the messages in the card that her friends in her tutor group had written to her. I could tell from what people had said that she was a popular girl.

'So many people are missing you, Louisa, and they want you to get well soon and go back to school,' I told her as I stroked her hand.

I wondered if she could hear me. What on earth must she be thinking? Probably, who was this woman and where on earth were her parents? I also wondered, even if she did wake up, what would she remember?

FOUR

Frozen in Time

By the time I got home that evening, I was exhausted. Even though Louisa wasn't physically living with me, the placement had officially started. Every evening I had to write up my record of the day and email it to Social Services, letting them know if there were any updates from the hospital and how Louisa was doing and any other information that I felt was relevant.

I'd just pressed the 'send' button on my email when Brian, Louisa's social worker, called.

'I'm sorry it's so late, Maggie, but it's been one of those days,' he told me. 'How did it go at the hospital?'

'I must admit it was a bit of a shock at first,' I told him. 'It was pretty harrowing to see how badly injured Louisa is.'

But I described how kind the ICU nurses were and that they had talked me through everything.

'I completely understand,' Brian replied. 'I went to visit her a few days ago before the placement meeting and it is upsetting. But so far she's responding well and we have to hope that she will get through this.'

I told him how the hospital had agreed to keep me updated and that I would pass anything on to him. I also let him know that I'd bought Louisa some things and had spoken to her school friends.

'Her hospital room looks a bit less bare now and she's got some essentials for when she wakes up,' I told him.

'It does feel a bit strange talking to someone who can't respond,' I added. 'I don't even know if she can hear me but I suppose I'll get used to it.'

'Well, it sounds like you're doing all the right things,' replied Brian.

Over the next few days, I was determined to do some research into how to help people in comas. I felt helpless so I was willing to try anything that might make a difference to Louisa and aid her recovery.

'Talking of Louisa's things,' said Brian, 'I had a call from DC Jenkins today. He's happy to organise a PC to meet you at Louisa's house so you can go in and collect some of Louisa's clothes and personal items. Could you do tomorrow?'

'Yes, that would be great,' I replied.

'All he's asked is that you note down anything that you take so there's a record of it in case anyone queries it further down the line.'

'Of course,' I said.

I wanted to get some things to take to Louisa at the hospital, but I also wanted to start getting a room ready for her at my house. It was always a lot easier for children to settle if they had some of their own familiar things around them. Admittedly, we didn't know if and when she would be discharged from hospital, but I was determined to stay positive and I always liked to be prepared.

Brian said he'd passed my number on and sure enough, DC Jenkins messaged me ten minutes after I put the phone down.

He sent me the address of the house and I arranged to meet his colleague PC Ridley there at 9 a.m.

Louisa's family home was a forty-five-minute drive from my house. Ideally, Social Services would try to place a child with a foster carer who was within a twenty-mile radius so there could be continuity with nurseries or schools. However, this wasn't always possible if they couldn't find a suitable foster carer with space. Also, sometimes it wasn't advisable if they were worried a child could potentially be at risk of harm from their biological parents and in those cases, it was seen as best if the child was placed with a carer in another county so there was no chance of bumping into their birth families. As I pulled into a street of Victorian terraced houses the next morning, I could see a uniformed police officer already waiting outside the red door of number 33.

He gave me a wave.

'PC Ridley?' I asked. 'Hi, I'm Maggie.'

I showed him my ID.

'Would you like me to come in with you?' he said. 'Or I'm happy to wait outside if you'd prefer to go in on your own?'

He had to wait to make sure the property was properly secured after I'd been in it. For now, as the family's next of kin was in Australia, the police had kept hold of the keys.

'I don't mind going in on my own,' I told him. 'I probably won't be too long. I just want to pick up a few personal items for the couple's daughter so she has some of her own things around her in the hospital.'

He nodded and handed me the keys.

'I'll wait in the car so just give me a shout if you need anything,' he said.

'Thank you.'

I unlocked the front door and pushed it open. It went straight into a living room. Ahead of me I could see a dining room with a round table and four chairs leading to a galley kitchen.

It was eerily quiet and it felt odd being in a stranger's house without them being there. It wasn't a big house but it had a nice energy about it and I could tell it was a well-loved family home.

I walked through to the kitchen and looked around, trying to get a feel for the people who had lived there. There were letters stuck to the fridge with magnets – reminders of school open evenings, dates of gymnastic competitions and a party invite for Louisa.

It felt like Louisa and her parents had just popped out. There were still cereal bowls and spoons soaking in the sink from the morning that they had left and a half-drunk cup of congealed tea in a 'Best Mum' mug on the side. I noticed the brand-new dog bed in the corner of the kitchen filled with dog toys.

On the worktop in the kitchen there was a hairbrush and a couple of bobbles on top of a puppy training handbook. I imagined Louisa that morning, only a week ago, filled with excitement about going to collect their new puppy.

'How life can suddenly change in a instant,' I thought to myself.

I knew I wasn't there to clean up but I couldn't just leave the dishes going mouldy in the sink and I noticed that the kitchen bin had started to smell too. I went back outside to where PC Ridley was waiting and tapped on the window of his car.

'Do you have any objections if I wash up some dirty dishes in the kitchen and clear up a bit?' I asked as he wound down his window. 'There's food going off in there and I don't want to leave it like that.'

'Not at all,' he replied. 'It's not like it's a crime scene or anything. I'll come and give you a hand.'

PC Ridley emptied the bins while I washed and dried up the breakfast things and wiped down the surfaces. I rummaged under the sink and found some bin bags then I cleared out the fridge of stuff that was about to go off or was already mouldy.

'That's much better,' I smiled. 'Thanks for your help.'

PC Ridley took the rubbish out while I got on with sorting out some stuff for Louisa.

I wandered into the living room and over to the sideboard, which was covered in family photos. There was a photo of Karen and Simon on their wedding day, a picture of a newborn Louisa fast asleep in her proud parents' arms. Chubby toddler Louisa sat on a beach with a bucket and spade, and a nervous-looking four-year-old Louisa with her hair in plaits wearing a school uniform that was much too big for her. I picked up one of the three of them together that looked like it had been taken more recently, on holiday at some sort of zoo or theme park. They were all in shorts, T-shirts and sun hats. Louisa and her dad both had a parrot sitting on their shoulder. Simon didn't look too pleased about it and Louisa and her mum, Karen, were cracking up. They were all pink from the sun with their mouths open, laughing. They all looked so happy.

I noticed that Louisa had the same long dark hair as her mum and had her dad's blue eyes.

As I looked at those three smiling faces in the picture, I felt an overwhelming feeling of sadness. A whole family had been ripped to shreds in seconds. The laughing teenager, who was almost as tall as her mother, looked so different to the bruised, swollen girl lying in a hospital bed attached to machines that were helping to keep her alive. All of that while her poor parents were lying in the morgue.

Life was just so cruel sometimes.

I took that photo and the wedding picture and put them in the suitcase that I'd brought with me and made a note of them on a list. It would be nice for Louisa to have a family photograph by her bedside in the ICU although I was aware it would also serve as a reminder of everything that she'd lost.

It didn't feel right going through their home, sorting through their stuff, but I reminded myself I was doing it with good intentions.

Afterwards I headed upstairs. There was a double bedroom, which was obviously Karen and Simon's, a smaller box room full of Karen's hairdressing equipment and supplies, and the back bedroom, which was clearly Louisa's. It was a typical teenage room – piles of clothes on the floor, a messy desk covered in school books and papers and a shelf full of gymnastics medals and trophies. It looked like blue was her favourite colour as everything was blue, from the colour of the paint on the walls to the duvet cover on the bed. I walked over to a huge noticeboard that was covered in photographs. I recognised the smiling faces of her friends, Becky, Phoenix and Frankie, who I'd met at the school yesterday, the three of them looking a lot younger and more baby-faced on their last day of primary school, their arms around each other and their white shirts covered in the signatures of their classmates. In another one they looked more grown up and glamorous, perhaps ready for a party. There were a few funny photos of Karen and Simon on there and one of Louisa with an older woman who I assumed was her grandmother.

I carefully unpinned a few photos off the noticeboard, put them in the case and added them to the list.

Underneath a mirror on the wall that was strewn with fairy lights was a jewellery box and a make-up bag. I put both straight into the suitcase as I knew how important those kinds of things were for teenagers.

Then I went through Louisa's wardrobe and drawers and put together a pile of clothes on the bed. I didn't know when I would be able to go into the house again so I chose quite a few things, from jeans and tops to leggings, underwear and shoes. I also put in a blue fleecy dressing gown and some striped cotton pyjamas. Louisa was currently in a hospital gown but I thought it would be nice when she woke up to be in her own clothes. I made sure it was all neatly folded as I packed it into the suitcase.

I noticed a couple of books lying open on her bedside table. They were both horror-type novels. I put a piece of paper in each of them to keep the pages and added them to the case.

I also took the duvet cover and pillow off her bed – I hoped that the familiar smell of home would help stir something in her subconscious. At the bottom of her bed, there was a small pile of soft toys. Most of them looked like the kind of things you won at fairgrounds but my eyes were drawn to a bedraggled-looking teddy. Its fur was all matted and it looked like the kind of well-loved toy that Louisa might have had since she was a baby so I popped it into the case too.

As I lugged the full suitcase across the landing, I glanced into Karen and Simon's room. There were still clothes on a chair and the bed was unmade. I noticed the bottle of Chanel No5 on top of the chest of drawers and lots more baby photos of Louisa. I knew this would all have to be cleared at some point but that wasn't my job today and somehow it didn't feel right going into their room.

I said goodbye to PC Ridley and put the case in the car.

'Thanks for all your help,' I told him.

I sat outside for a few minutes after he left, staring at the red front door and wondering when I would next be back here. I had everything crossed that it would be with Louisa.

As soon as I got home, I started sorting. I went through the case and hung up Louisa's clothes in one of the bedrooms that I used for fostering. As I had no other children living with me at the moment, I gave her the larger of the two rooms, which had a bunk bed as well as a single bed in it. I didn't want to unpack for her so I sorted out the things I was going to take up to the hospital that afternoon – her teddy, the photographs, some books and the dressing gown and pyjamas.

By mid-afternoon I was sat back in ICU. There was a different charge nurse on duty today.

'How's she been?' I asked her.

'There's nothing of note to tell you really,' the nurse told me. 'She's still in a stable condition and she's had a settled night and morning.'

I explained that I'd brought a few things from home for Louisa.

'Would it be OK to put a few photos on the walls?' I asked.

'Yes, of course,' she said. 'Anything is fine as long as it doesn't interfere with any of the equipment.'

This visit, I had plenty to keep me busy. I got some Blu-tack and attached some of the photos of Louisa and her friends to the side of the cupboard next to her bed.

'This is a lovely one of you, Becky, Phoenix and Frankie,' I told her. 'You're all dressed up and you look like you're going to a party. The girls send their love and hope you're back at school soon.'

I put the framed family picture and the wedding photo of Karen and Simon on top of the cupboard next to the faux sunflowers that I'd bought the previous day.

'It's such a lovely one of your parents,' I said aloud. 'They look so happy.'

I was careful not to mention anything about the crash and what had happened to them. It didn't feel right. No one truly understood what she could or couldn't hear or understand but I didn't want to risk her hearing something as traumatic as that.

I chatted away to Louisa as I put the dressing gown and pyjamas inside the cupboard along with the toiletries that I'd got her.

'And I had to bring you this teddy,' I continued. 'I found him on your bed and he looks like a very well-loved little chap, so I thought he'd make a nice friend for the Jelly Cat bunny.'

In my past experience, even teenagers still got comfort from soft toys when they were feeling ill, scared or vulnerable.

After I'd found a place for everything, I took one of the books that I'd found by her bed and started to read

44

to her. Even though the story was some hideous tale about teenage girls who kept getting murdered, there was something incredibly soothing about reading out loud and I was enjoying it.

'I hope you can hear me, Louisa, and you're enjoying this,' I told her.

But the only response I got were the endless bleeps of the machines.

Wendy, the nurse whom I'd met the day before, had just started her shift and she came in to see me.

'Ooh it's looking really lovely in here,' she smiled, as she looked around the room.

'I thought I'd try and cheer things up a bit,' I smiled.

'Well, you've done a great job,' she replied. 'It's nice for patients to have their own things around them. It can also be nice for visitors to get involved in their care.'

She explained that she'd come to give Louisa a wash.

'You can do it if you like,' she told me. 'It's just her face this time.'

'OK,' I said.

She passed me a sponge and a bowl of warm water and left me to it.

I could see her dark hair under her bandage and her dark eyelashes. She was a beautiful girl.

I gently patted the lacerations on her cheeks that had scabbed over and cleaned around her eyes and ears. Her physical scars were starting to heal but I knew the emotional ones would run a lot deeper.

Then I patted her lips and smoothed down her dark hair.

'Come on,' I whispered. 'You can do this. I know that

you're in there somewhere, Louisa. You can do this. You can pull through and get better.'

I desperately hoped that somehow she could hear me and that my pleas would come true.

FIVE

Rude Awakenings

Time passed and I started to get used to the new routine. Every day, I'd head up to the hospital and spend a few hours sitting at Louisa's bedside in the ICU.

Sometimes I read to her or had Radio 1 playing quietly in the background. Other times I helped the nurses to wash her and they showed me how to gently massage her hands and arms to try to help her joints to stay flexible.

I chatted away to her about all sorts of things, from school, gymnastics and her friends to the weather and world events if I was really struggling. But there was always one topic missing from my conversation – the car crash and what had happened to her parents.

Louisa had been in a coma for nearly ten days now and so far, nothing had changed.

'Should we be worried that she's not responding or waking up?' I asked Wendy while she was changing Louisa's IV fluids one day.

'Unfortunately it's the unknown,' she told me. 'Comas can last from days to weeks or even months. It's her body's way of giving her brain time to heal. I know it's hard but all you can do is be patient.'

I'd never experienced a placement like it before and it was odd chatting to someone who never answered back.

Louisa didn't live with me, I'd never heard her voice or had a proper conversation with her – all I knew about her was from what other people had told me. Yet already I felt fiercely protective towards her. Her parents weren't here any more and I was the only person that she had looking out for her.

She was the first thought on my mind every morning and the last one at night because I knew if she woke up, she was going to have to face the worst news imaginable but I desperately wanted her to live and to help her get through this.

On the way home from the hospital one night, I popped into Vicky's for a chat.

'How are you doing?' she asked me. 'You look shattered, Maggie.'

'I don't know why because I'm not really doing anything,' I replied. 'It's tiring in a strange way.'

Sitting for hours on end in a small hospital room thinking about how to entertain someone who was unconscious was surprisingly draining.

'I can imagine,' said Vicky. 'It must be very intense. Everything is on you to make conversation but you're not getting anything back. And time always seems to drag in those places.'

I told her how it reminded me of the times that I'd fostered babies who had been in the neonatal unit to begin with. That endless feeling of fear and anticipation as you walked through the hospital to the unit, terrified that something had happened and that you were going to be greeted with bad news. Time dragged but spending hours not doing a lot in a stuffy hospital ward would still mean that you felt exhausted and drained when you left.

'It's mainly about me finding things to do to make me feel useful and keep me busy,' I said.

Every day I'd make sure Louisa's hospital room was clean and tidy and I'd wipe down surfaces.

I'd just got in from Vicky's that night when I had a call from a woman called Margaret. She explained that she was the mum of Louisa's friend, Frankie.

'Miss Grey passed on your number,' she told me. 'I know the other girls' parents aren't keen but Frankie would really like to go and visit Louisa at the hospital.'

I know I'd suggested it but I was now in two minds about whether it was actually a good idea.

'Are you sure?' I asked her. 'Frankie got quite upset when I was talking to them about Louisa at school the other day.'

I explained that it was quite harrowing to see her.

'She's covered in tubes and wires and she's very bruised and swollen,' I warned. 'I just don't want Frankie to be traumatised or upset by it.'

'She seems determined and I think it would help her come to terms with what's happened,' Margaret insisted.

So I arranged to be at the hospital towards the end of the week when Margaret would bring Frankie after school.

If I was being honest, all the days had started to merge into one as there was nothing to differentiate them from each other. Even though it felt like much longer, it had only been a week since baby Micah had left to go and live with his new adoptive parents. Dionne messaged me every few days and, much to my relief, things seemed to be going smoothly. Micah had settled well and I could tell they all adored him. We'd had a couple of chats on the phone too and when she'd asked, I'd told her about my new placement. I hadn't gone into detail for confidentiality reasons but I'd said I was fostering a young girl who was currently in hospital in a coma.

'Gosh, poor thing,' she had sighed. 'That must be hard.'

Brian was also calling me regularly for an update and one morning he popped round for a chat.

'How is everything going, Maggie?' he asked me as I made us a cup of tea.

'As well as it can be I suppose,' I replied.

We talked about my visits to the hospital and how Louisa was getting on.

'I think if things stay the same as they are now then certain decisions are going to have to be made,' Brian told me. 'I've been in touch with Martin, Simon's brother in Australia, and he needs to start organising her parents' funeral.'

The sad fact was, they couldn't hang on for months in the hope that Louisa would wake up.

'The other thing that Martin will have to do when he's over here is sort out his brother's house,' he added. 'It needs to be cleared and the keys need to be given back to the housing association by the end of next month.'

Having been to the house myself, I knew that would be a huge job. That house contained a whole life that needed to be sorted through. Louisa was trapped in this limbo but I understood that life had to carry on around her.

That afternoon, Frankie was coming to the hospital after school to visit Louisa. I met her and Margaret by the doors to the ICU.

'Nice to see you again,' I told her. 'It's really lovely that you wanted to come and visit Louisa.'

She looked really nervous and, as we walked down the corridor, I tried to prepare her.

'Remember that Louisa doesn't look how she normally does,' I told her gently. 'She was in a really bad crash so she's very swollen and bruised and she's hurt her leg.'

I also warned her about the machines.

'There's a lot of bleeping, which drives me mad,' I smiled. 'But the doctors and the nurses need these machines to check how she's doing. They keep an eye on all the important things like her heart rate.'

Frankie nodded.

'It's OK, I've seen stuff like that on TV shows,' she said.

But this was real life. Not something on a screen.

When we finally got to Louisa's room, Frankie hesitated outside the doorway.

'Are you sure you want to do this, sweetie?' Margaret asked and Frankie nodded bravely.

'Hi Louisa,' I said loudly as we walked in. 'I've brought someone very special to see you today.'

Frankie looked apprehensive as she walked towards the bed.

'Can I talk to her?' she asked me. 'Do you think she can hear me?'

'No one knows for sure but I think it's worth a try,' I smiled. 'I talk to her all the time; in fact, she's probably sick of the sound of my voice.'

I pulled up a chair closer to Louisa's bed for her while Margaret and I sat on the sidelines.

'That poor girl,' she sighed.

Frankie was really brave and chatted away to her. She told her all the gossip from school, who was going out with who, who'd got into trouble, and the parties and sleepovers they'd been to.

'Can I touch her?' she asked me.

'Of course,' I nodded.

She held her hand.

'Please wake up, Lou Lou,' she begged her. 'We all miss you loads and next month is Phoenix's birthday and she's going to have a party. It won't be the same without you. Please get better.'

I could see that Margaret was getting upset.

'Why don't me and your mum go and get a cup of tea from the vending machine while you stay with Louisa?' I suggested. 'We'll only be two minutes.'

'Is that alright with you, sweetheart?' Margaret asked Frankie.

She nodded.

Margaret and I walked down the corridor.

'Thank you,' she told me. 'It was all getting a bit much for me in there. I just keep thinking about Louisa and her poor parents.'

'Did you know them well?' I asked her.

'Not really,' she sighed. 'The girls went to different primary schools but I'd met Karen a few times when I'd picked Frankie up from their house. She seemed like a lovely woman. It's just so sad.'

'It really is,' I agreed.

I'd just fed some money into the vending machine when suddenly we heard a loud shriek. I knew instinctively it was Frankie.

So did Margaret. She ran down the corridor in a panic with me swiftly following behind her.

'What is it, love?' she asked Frankie.

'Louisa opened her eyes, Mum!' she gasped. 'I was talking to her and she opened her eyes and stared at me.'

I looked down at the bed. Louisa's eyes were firmly closed as if they had been the entire time.

'Are you sure, Frankie?' asked Margaret.

'I swear, Mum,' sighed Frankie. 'She opened them and looked right at me.'

'Well, that's wonderful isn't it, Maggie?' asked Margaret. 'That must be a good sign?'

'I think so,' I shrugged. 'Although I have read that people in comas sometimes make involuntary movements that they're not aware of.'

I didn't want to accuse Frankie of lying but I also thought it might be a case of wishful thinking.

'She looked right at me,' said Frankie proudly. 'Louisa heard my voice and she knew it was me.'

It was true that Frankie's was the first familiar voice that Louisa had heard since she'd been in a coma. So maybe it had happened?

'I'll go and mention it to the nurses,' I said.

I went and told Wendy what Frankie had seen.

'I've noticed her eyelids fluttering before but I've never seen her fully open her eyes,' I said.

'We haven't seen her do that but if she did, that's a really good sign,' she told me. 'We'll keep a lookout.'

For the rest of the visit, Louisa's eyes remained closed and over the next few days, everything remained exactly the same. It had been nice to have a flicker of hope but I started to believe that if Frankie had seen anything, it was an involuntary movement that Louisa had no control of.

One morning, I was doing a bit of cleaning before I was due to head to the hospital when my phone rang.

'Hi, it's Deborah here,' said a voice. 'I'm the senior charge nurse on ICU today.'

I felt panic rising in my chest. This was the first time the hospital had called me at home.

'What is it?' I asked. 'What's happened? How's Louisa?'

'She's absolutely fine,' she told me. 'In fact, I was ringing to tell you that she's started to show some signs that she's coming out of her coma.'

'What?' I gasped. 'Really? That's wonderful! What kind of signs? Has she said anything?'

I had so many questions.

The charge nurse described how last night she had briefly opened her eyes and looked around.

'This morning she did it again,' she said. 'The nurse said she had her eyes open for around ten minutes, which is obviously a really positive sign. The consultant would like to have a chat with you later on today about everything if that's possible?'

'Yes, of course,' I said.

I told her that I was heading up to the hospital shortly.

'Would it be OK to notify Louisa's social worker as I'm sure he would like to attend too?'

'Absolutely,' she replied. 'I was about to give him a call myself.'

For the first time in weeks, I felt hope that things were changing. I felt guilty that I had doubted what Frankie had said she'd seen.

The ICU consultant, Mr Edwards, couldn't see us until later on that day, but I decided to go up to the hospital as planned to see Louisa first.

As I drove there, I felt a strange mixture of emotions. I was so pleased that it looked like Louisa was coming out of her coma but also I dreaded telling her about her parents. Now she was hopefully starting to come round, one of her first questions was surely going to be where were her parents? What if that was today? I knew it was something that Brian and I needed to discuss ASAP. She'd want to know why there were no familiar faces around her bed.

I felt a real sense of anticipation as I walked down the corridor of ICU and into Louisa's room. But my heart sank when I saw her lying in bed, her eyes closed, with the bleeping of the usual machines. I don't know what I had been expecting but it looked like nothing had changed.

'Hi Louisa,' I told her, giving her hand a squeeze. 'It's Maggie here. I hope you had a settled night.'

I waited with bated breath for some sort of response or reaction. But there was nothing.

When one of the nurses came in, I asked her about it.

'The charge nurse called me earlier and said she had started to wake up,' I told her. 'But she looks exactly the same.'

'I'm afraid it's not like in the films or on TV,' the nurse told me gently. 'People generally come out of comas very gradually. They don't tend to suddenly wake up and immediately start chatting and walking around – it can be a long process.'

She explained that Louisa had opened her eyes for a few minutes this morning.

'I was checking her vitals and her gaze followed me across the room, which is such an encouraging sign,' she said. 'Hopefully she'll start to do that more and more over the coming days as she becomes more conscious.'

It made me realise how little I knew.

Later that afternoon I went to meet Brian at the door of the ICU.

'How is she?' he asked. 'Has she said anything?'

I explained that she seemed exactly the same.

'Hopefully the consultant will tell us more,' I sighed.

The charge nurse directed us to a small room at the side of the ward where Mr Edwards was waiting.

He was a tall, grey-haired man in his fifties, who had a calm, gentle manner that meant you instantly trusted him.

'Thanks for coming in,' he said. 'The great news is that Louisa is showing some slight improvements and I wanted to talk you through that. Unfortunately it isn't as simple as regaining consciousness and waking up,' he explained. 'There are varying levels of coma. Everyone is different and recovery can be very gradual with some people.'

He explained that it was possible that initially Louisa would only be awake for a few minutes a day.

'She might not have any understanding or awareness and,' he said. 'When they first wake up, patients can also become very agitated. Sometimes they have hallucinations and it can be really distressing for them.'

'Do you know when she'll be able to talk?' asked Brian.

Mr Edwards held out his hands.

'It's impossible to tell,' he told us. 'She probably won't be able to respond to you initially. We'll just have to see how she goes over the next few days.'

He also had a warning for us.

'One thing I would say is that we still don't know exactly how the crash has affected Louisa's brain. She might wake up and have a full recovery or there might be some things that she has problems with and has to relearn.'

He pointed out that it could be things like walking and talking.

'Could she have sustained permanent damage?' asked Brian.

'Maybe,' Mr Edwards replied. 'The other thing you need to be prepared for is that she might never regain full consciousness.'

He explained that although some patients weren't in a coma any more, they never regained full awareness or understanding. 'So Louisa might open her eyes and look around,' he said, 'but that might be it – that might be where the progress stops.'

Some patients were left in what was known as a vegetative state or minimally conscious.

It was becoming clear that there were rarely Hollywood endings when it came to brain injuries and comas. I had naively assumed that Louisa would either live or die but there were so many unknown levels in between. I had been feeling so positive but now we had to face facts. Louisa might make a full recovery or equally she might be left in a vegetative state or profoundly disabled. No one knew or could give us any answers; no one could tell us what the future held and that was really hard. All we could do was hold onto the hope that, against all the odds, Louisa would make a full recovery.

SIX

Fear of the Unknown

I kept going over and over what Mr Edwards had said. My whole focus had been on Louisa staying alive. But even if she did survive, there were clearly so many variations of what her recovery and life might look like that I hadn't considered or even been aware of.

The reality was, at some point, the doctors might say this was as much progress as she was going to make. She was breathing on her own but she would possibly still need tube feeding and 24-hour care and wouldn't be able to do anything herself. Maybe eventually she'd be able to move her eyes or blink but as Mr Edwards had warned us, that could be it.

'That feels like an existence rather than a life,' I told Anna, my supervising social worker, when I gave her a call that night to discuss my fears. 'I hadn't realised any of this when I took on this placement.'

'None of us did, Maggie,' she replied.

All sorts of doubts and worries had crept into my mind after our conversation with the consultant. If Louisa was left severely brain-damaged or in a minimal state of consciousness, in reality could I give her the specialist care that she needed?

I knew a couple of foster carers who specialised in fostering profoundly disabled babies and children or those with life-limiting conditions. Their houses were set up for it and were wheelchair-accessible and filled with all sorts of equipment. My friend Angela's front room had a hospital bed in it and there were oxygen machines, hoists and a downstairs bathroom. Even with adaptations, I wasn't sure if there was room in my terraced house with its narrow stairs.

'You have to be an incredibly committed, special person to do that kind of fostering,' I told Anna.

It was physically and emotionally demanding and I wasn't sure that I'd be able to cope with it. I thought about the main reason I had started to foster – to help children move forwards.

I knew that it possibly sounded selfish but I had to be honest, for both my sake and Louisa's. I was starting to question whether I was the right person for the job.

'It's clear that whatever happens, Louisa's recovery is going to be slow and uncertain,' said Anna. 'So the question now is, do you want to carry on when everything is so unknown?'

'I'm not sure but I can't bear the thought of giving up on her,' I sighed. 'She's doesn't have anyone.'

'Everyone would understand,' Anna told me. 'It's better to voice your concerns now rather than six months down the line when Louisa's living with you and you realise that you can't cope. It's not about being selfish, it's about being realistic,' she continued. 'Yes, fostering is a job but it's also your life. You don't just do nine to five then leave it at the office. It's a 24/7 commitment and you have to be sure that you can cope with these scenarios.'

I had to be honest with myself. I would never say no to a child in need and I felt so protective towards Louisa, but could I physically manage her and her potential future needs? Was this what I wanted my fostering to be, for the next few years? Could I cope with it all as a single carer?

'The flip side of the coin is, she could also make a full recovery,' Anna told me. 'It might take time but she could get back to how she was before the crash.'

The problem was, none of us knew.

'I wish I had a crystal ball so I could see into the future,' I sighed.

'It sounds like you've got a lot of thinking to do, Maggie,' Anna said kindly. 'It's Friday today. Why don't you have a couple of days off from visiting Louisa over the weekend and just take some time to work out whether to carry on with the placement?'

'I can't do that,' I gasped. 'What if something happens?'

'The hospital has got your number and they can call you if they need you,' she told me. 'I'll let Brian know what's happening. Let's see how you feel on Monday and have a chat then,' she said.

'OK,' I sighed.

I spent most of the weekend in turmoil. I didn't know Louisa; I had never heard her voice. But I still felt protective of her and had a deep sense of loyalty to her. However, was it fair to carry on with the placement if I was having doubts? I knew that if I couldn't care for her, then someone else could.

Even though I wasn't physically at the hospital, I couldn't stop thinking about her.

'How is she?' I asked as I called the ICU for the third time that day.

'Maggie, Louisa is fine,' Deborah, the senior charge nurse, reassured me. 'She's comfortable and there's nothing more to tell you. There have been no developments.'

I wondered if it would set her recovery back if I wasn't there to talk to her and read to her. I knew how dedicated and caring the staff were; they did their best, but it was a busy unit and they were always rushed off their feet.

By Monday morning, I was sure of my answer.

'How was the weekend, Maggie?' Anna asked when she called. 'Did you manage to switch off and relax?'

'To be honest, no not at all,' I laughed. 'But it did make my decision easy for me.'

'Well you always do know your mind,' she teased. 'What did you decide?'

'I'm going to continue with the placement,' I said firmly. 'I can't give up on her, Anna. She needs me.'

It felt like there was a long, uncertain road ahead of us but Louisa and I would travel it together. No one knew what the future held but I would be there by her side to help her through it. She'd already had such terrible loss in her life; there was no way that I could knowingly walk away and leave her. Even though we didn't know each other and she couldn't respond to me yet, I already cared deeply about her. I'd invested time in her and I felt like I was already committed to her and her future, whatever that might be.

'Things change so quickly and we'll just have to take it each day as it comes,' I shrugged.

After a couple of days away, I couldn't wait to get back to the hospital to see her.

'Hi Maggie, we've missed you,' Wendy grinned as I walked down the ward.

'How's she been?' I asked her.

'Good as gold,' she told me.

As I walked into her room, it was reassuring to hear the machines bleeping away and to see that Louisa was comfortable.

'I've brought you a new book, Louisa,' I told her. 'And, according to the reviews, this is the best one yet. We might even find out who the murderer is this time. Let's see, shall we?'

I'd already read her the two books that I'd found on her bedside table. They were both from the same series so I'd bought the third and final one in the trilogy.

'I hope you're paying attention, young lady,' I joked. 'Right, if you're sitting comfortably then I'll begin.'

After I'd finished the first couple of pages, I glanced up at Louisa and did a double take.

Much to my astonishment, her eyes were wide open and she was staring up at the ceiling.

I held my breath, unsure of what to do. Should I call a nurse? I decided not to as I didn't want to risk her closing them again if I left the room. Should I talk to her?

I patted her hand.

'Louisa, if you don't know this already then I'm Maggie,' I told her. 'I did introduce myself a few weeks ago when we first met but I thought I'd better tell you again just in case you don't remember. Mine is the annoying voice that you hear in your ear every day.'

I watched in utter amazement as she slowly turned her head to one side to face me.

'Hello there, flower,' I said, grinning. 'It's so lovely to see you.'

I stared into her eyes, which were the same piercing blue as her dad Simon's.

'You're doing so well,' I told her. 'I hope you're starting to feel better.'

I was willing her to respond, but, although she was looking straight at me, her eyes were glassy and I wasn't sure if there was any recognition there.

'Shall I carry on reading?' I asked her. 'I think you must be enjoying this new book.'

I started another chapter. As I read, I kept looking up and her gaze was still focused on me. I got through five chapters before her eyes closed again.

It felt like a huge milestone. It was as if she knew that I needed a sign to show me that she was improving.

I went out to the nurses' desk to tell them what had happened.

'That's the first time I've seen her with her eyes fully open,' I told the senior charge nurse, Claire.

'Hopefully it will happen more and more and for longer periods of time as she becomes more alert,' she replied.

That night I couldn't wait to get home and call Anna to tell her the good news.

'That's amazing, Maggie,' she told me. 'It must have been really wonderful for you to see.'

'It was,' I replied. 'There's still a long way to go but I feel like slowly she's coming back to us.'

I also made a note of what had happened in my daily recordings and sent them to Brian.

Over the next few days, progress was rapid. Louisa's eyes were open for longer periods and she would follow people around the room.

But she still wasn't speaking or moving.

'Hopefully that will come in time,' Wendy reassured me.

I wondered what Louisa must be thinking as she lay there, watching us. Did she remember that she'd been in an accident? Did she even understand where she was?

At the back of my mind, I still remembered what Mr Edwards had told us. I knew there was a big risk that she would never get past this stage. She might have come out of the coma but she could be trapped in this state, never fully gaining consciousness or being able to communicate or understand the world around her. We just had to hope that she would keep progressing.

As the days passed, other little things started to happen. Her arms started to move a little bit and once, when Wendy was moving her to help prevent pressure sores, she moaned.

'Did that hurt, sweetheart?' she asked her. 'I'm trying to be as gentle as I can but we've got to keep changing your position.'

When Frankie's mum, Margaret, messaged me to say that Frankie wanted to come and visit again, I was delighted.

'I'm so pleased you came back,' I told her when she arrived at the hospital. 'Ever since you came to visit, Louisa's been opening her eyes more and more.'

'Does that mean she's getting better?' Frankie asked.

'We really hope so,' I said.

When Frankie walked in, Louisa was lying in bed with her eyes open.

Frankie beamed when she saw her. She sat down on the chair next to her bed.

'Hi Lou Lou,' she said. 'I knew you'd get better. I knew when you opened your eyes the last time that you'd heard me. Phoenix and Becky say hi. We all miss you so much.'

'Maggie, look,' she said softly. 'She's crying.'

I looked over at the bed and, sure enough, she was. Louisa's eyes were open and she was staring at the ceiling but there were tears leaking out of them onto her pillow. I'd never been so happy to see someone cry before.

'I'm sorry, Louisa,' Frankie told her. 'I didn't mean to upset you.'

She wasn't making any noise but I was convinced they were genuine tears. I now felt certain that Louisa was in there somewhere and that she had some awareness.

Later that week, Mr Edwards came to see me on the ward.

'Can we have a chat?' he asked.

'Of course,' I said, following him out of Louisa's room and into one of the visitor rooms off the ward.

'I believe Lousia has been showing some progress,' he said.

'Yes, she's opened her eyes and she's been watching us as well as moving. And the other day one of her best friends came to visit her and she cried. They're all good signs, right? She's definitely coming out of her coma?'

He explained that a coma was when someone was unconscious and unresponsive.

'If someone's in a coma, they don't move, they don't talk, they don't do anything. One of the things that defines a coma is that the eyes are closed. So in all those respects, I agree, Louisa is coming out of her coma.

'She's definitely more reactive and responsive,' he continued. 'So she's moved to a place that we'd describe more as a vegetative state.'

'She's not in a vegetative state,' I said, horrified. 'She's coming round. I can tell. She's looking around and she's moving a bit and making noises. She got upset when she saw her friend Frankie – so she can show emotion. That's not someone who's a vegetable.'

Mr Edwards reminded me that someone in a vegetative state could still do all of those things.

'They can move a little, open their eyes, look around and make noises – they can even laugh or cry,' he explained. 'They're responding but not in a meaningful way. So if I banged that door, for example, Louisa might jump because the noise has startled her but she won't understand that what caused the noise was the door.'

I was convinced that she was more aware than that.

'Is there a scan you can do to show that she's definitely coming round to full consciousness?'

Mr Edwards shook his head.

'I wish there was as it would make my job much easier,' he sighed. 'There's no scan that can show that. It's just a case of observing someone over time.'

He told me that there was one test that he liked to do.

'We can do it now if you want?' he asked and I nodded eagerly.

I followed him back into Louisa's room. She was lying there, propped up slightly with her eyes open although she didn't show any reaction.

'Hello Louisa,' he told her. 'I'm the ICU consultant, Mr Edwards, but everyone calls me Jim. It's great to see you with your eyes open.'

Then suddenly, without any warning, he bent down and pinched the skin on the top of her right hand. Louisa jumped in surprise and immediately pushed his hand away.

'I'm sorry about that, Louisa,' he said. 'I bet you think I'm really mean but I was just testing your reactions.'

We walked back outside.

'That was a really good sign,' he told me, but went on to explain that even if she was in a vegetative state, Louisa could still feel pain and might have still jumped if he had pinched her.

'It would have just been her reflexes working,' he said. 'But the fact that she jumped and then went to swipe my hand away tells me there is a level of awareness there. She understood that not only did it hurt but that it was me and my hand that had caused the pain,' he said. 'So that is a really positive sign.'

I knew there were no guarantees but it felt like a big step forward towards Louisa regaining full consciousness.

Another huge leap forwards came a few days later when I walked into the ward.

'Morning,' I smiled to Janet, one of the nurses. 'How she's been overnight?'

Janet smiled. 'I couldn't wait to tell you this but last night, she said her first word.'

'What?' I gasped. 'That's amazing news. What did she say?'

'She was asking for someone,' Janet told me.

My heart immediately sank. 'Was it her parents?' I asked.

She shook her head. 'No, it was someone called Luna. She said the same name two or three times.

'Luna?' I said, puzzled.

'Perhaps it's a friend of hers from school?' Janet suggested.

I hadn't heard anyone mention a Luna but, for some reason, it did sound familiar.

Suddenly it came to me.

'Oh it's the dog!' I gasped.

I explained that Luna was the name of the new puppy that they'd been to collect on the morning of the crash.

'Well that's a positive sign if she's retained a memory of that day,' she said.

It was so positive but it also filled me with dread. If Louisa remembered Luna, what else did she remember? Had she fallen unconscious straight away or did she remember every harrowing detail of the crash?

I was so relieved that, every day, her understanding and awareness was growing but I was also feeling anxious about what lay ahead. At some point, we were going to have to tell her what had happened to her parents and devastate her life – it felt like that inevitable moment was getting closer.

SEVEN

Progress

The weeks passed and Louisa's progress was very gradual. I was grateful for every little achievement but there were good days and bad ones.

She had moments of consciousness where she was looking around and watching what the nurses and I were doing. There were even times that she would smile at us when we spoke to her. But there were some times that, all she would do was sleep.

She was alert and awake one afternoon when Mr Edwards came to examine her.

'I'm going to see if she can respond to a few simple commands,' he told me.

He got out a little torch and got her to follow the beam of light with her eyes, which she did easily.

'Louisa, if you can hear me, I'd like you to blink twice for yes,' he asked her.

I waited, desperately willing her on. It would be amazing if we had some way of communicating with her, even on a basic level.

Her blue eyes stared into space.

Nothing.

'Please blink twice if you can hear me,' Mr Edwards repeated.

Suddenly Louisa's eyelids started to flutter.

I held my breath.

Then, very slowly, her eyes closed and then opened again.

Once.

Then twice.

'Clever girl!' I exclaimed. 'That's incredible!'

'Well done,' said Mr Edwards. 'I'm going to try something a bit more complicated now.'

'Louisa, I want you to touch your left ear for me and then your right ear.'

I knew this would be hard for her as, even if she understood what the consultant was asking, she'd lost so much muscle tone in the past few weeks and her arms were very weak and looked like skin and bone.

I could see the determination in Louisa's eyes as she desperately tried to lift her shaky left arm. She struggled to get it any further than a few inches off the bed until it flopped back down by her side.

'That's a really good effort, Louisa,' Mr Edwards told her. 'I could see that you were really trying there.'

Even though it was a struggle physically, it was clear that she knew what he wanted her to do.

'Maggie, I'd like you to take hold of Louisa's hand,' he told me.

'Louisa, if you can hear me, please squeeze Maggie's hand.'

I did as he'd asked and reached for Louisa's hand. It felt like a dead weight and her fingers were stiff and couldn't curl around mine.

She turned her head to look at me.

'Go on,' I encouraged. 'You can do it. Try to squeeze my hand.'

I smiled as I felt a very gentle pressure on my fingers. She didn't have the strength for a strong grip or to squeeze but it was a definite attempt.

'Well done,' I smiled. 'You're doing so well.'

As I looked at her, I could see the frustration in her eyes.

'Don't worry, you'll get there,' I reassured her.

To me, this felt like huge progress. Even though there were some things that she couldn't do yet physically, she had shown us that the understanding and the awareness was there. Her brain wasn't as damaged as perhaps we'd first feared.

'All good, positive signs,' smiled Mr Edwards as he got ready to move on to the next patient. 'I'll talk to occupational therapy and she can hopefully start having some physio to help build up her strength and her muscle tone.'

It was such a huge relief after all the weeks of uncertainty and I felt tears pricking my eyes. They were tears of pride and I desperately hoped that Louisa was going to keep improving and recover from all this, to be able to lead some semblance of a normal life rather than just existing.

Vicky's house was on the way home from the hospital so, as I often did, I called in there on my way back. It was good to be able to offload the events of the day onto someone.

'I feel like Louisa's definitely coming back to us,' I told Vicky as she made me a coffee. 'I'm convinced of it – I can see it just by looking at her. That glassy look in her eyes has gone and she seems more present somehow. I hadn't known her before all of this but I'm convinced that the real Louisa is in there and will come out.'

'That's great news, Maggie,' she replied.

'I was so worried that she would be stuck in a vegetative state so it's a relief to see her making progress and responding to more and more things,' I said.

'Do you think she understands who you are?' Vicky asked.

'I just don't know,' I shrugged. 'I keep reminding her that I'm Maggie and I'm a foster carer but I don't even know if she understand what that means. She's probably lying there thinking who the heck is this woman and why does she keep insisting on talking to me and playing the radio,' I chuckled.

In truth, I was constantly worried about how and when we were going to tell her about her parents.

'How do we know when the right time is?' I asked a few days later at a meeting at Social Services.

We were having a Looked After Child (LAC) review for Louisa. Even though she wasn't living with me yet, it was still important for everyone involved in her care to get together from time to time and talk about where we were at.

'Unfortunately Mr Edwards wasn't able to make it today to give us his input,' said Brian, Louisa's social worker. It was completely understandable given his job in intensive care medicine.

'However, I had a call with him the other day and we talked about telling Louisa,' he added. 'At this stage, he feels the priority is to keep Louisa calm and stable. She's making good progress but no one is 100 per cent sure what level her understanding is and we don't want that progress to stop.'

'I agree in that I don't feel that we can tell her such devastating news when we don't know how aware she is,' I nodded. 'But I do feel like the time will come soon when she needs to know. We will at least have to try to tell her.'

Whenever I went to visit Louisa, it always felt like the elephant in the room. I imagined that she was lying there wondering where her parents were and why they hadn't come to visit her. If that was the case, it must be excruciating for her not to be able to communicate that.

'I think it's something we need to address soon,' nodded Brian, 'but it just doesn't sit right with me to tell her about her parents when she can't talk to us or ask any questions.'

Louisa had only said one thing so far and that was asking for her puppy, Luna.

'Well we have to hope that her speech will be the next thing that comes back,' added Anna, my supervising social worker, who was also sitting in on the meeting. 'From what Maggie has told me, every day she's making more and more progress.'

I nodded.

'I think we just need to keep an eye on the situation,' agreed Brian.

He also informed us that the local authority was going to go for a full care order, meaning they would have full parental responsibility for Louisa.

'I've been speaking regularly to Louisa's uncle Martin and keeping him updated about everything that's happening here,' Brian told us. 'Being based in Australia, he doesn't feel that it's fair to make Louisa travel thousands of miles to be with a family member that she doesn't actually know.'

Brian had been to visit Louisa's grandma in her care home.

'Her dementia means that she's barely able to care for herself, let alone someone else,' he said sadly. 'Staff members have tried to tell her about the crash but her mental capacity means she can't remember or recognise her family let alone understand that her daughter and son-in-law have died and her granddaughter is seriously injured.'

It was all so very sad.

'The family did have friends and while everyone is concerned about Louisa, no one feels like they are able to take her on full time and offer her a home. Hence we're going to go for a full care order.'

I really did feel for Louisa. She was pretty much alone in the world and even though I was a stranger, I was the closest thing she had to a family now.

One morning, I headed up to the hospital as usual and asked the question that I always did when I arrived.

'How's she been overnight, Wendy?' I asked the nurse, as I walked down the ICU towards Louisa's room.

The answer was normally 'calm and settled' but this time, Wendy shook her head.

'She's been a bit of a handful actually,' she told me.

'Why, what happened?' I asked, surprised.

'Early this morning I heard someone shouting and when I went to check on her, she was trying to pull her IVs and her feeding tube out,' she told me. 'And when I tried to stop her, she tried to hit me.'

I was shocked as I didn't think Louisa had the strength for that and she'd never lashed out before.

'Oh no,' I said. 'That's awful, I'm so sorry.'

It didn't sound like the actions of the sweet, gentle girl that everyone had been telling me about.

'Oh don't worry, she didn't hurt me,' Wendy smiled. 'It's happened to me in the past with other coma patients. The poor lass was very agitated and confused,' she told me. 'She didn't seem to know where she was and she was quite distressed.'

She explained that, for her own safety, they'd had to restrain her.

'She's fine now,' she told me, 'although she's slept a lot since.'

I thought back to Mr Edwards' words. We had no idea how the coma or the crash had affected Louisa. It wasn't as simple as repairing broken bones. They could heal but the brain was a lot more complex.

Thankfully Louisa looked calm and when I walked in, she opened her eyes.

'Hello young lady,' I told her. 'Wendy's been telling me that you were being a little bit feisty this morning.'

I chatted away to her for a while.

'Right then, Louisa,' I said. 'Shall we do some reading?'

Her gaze followed me as I lent over to get the book out of the cupboard next to her bed.

When she saw what I was doing, Louisa started to blink furiously. Then she began to shake her head.

'What is it, flower?' I asked her. 'Don't you like this book?'

She blinked twice.

'Or do you not want me to read to you today?'

'Nnnnn,' she croaked.

I could see her lips moving as she struggled to get the words out.

'Nnnnn . . .'

'Are you trying to say "no"?' I asked her.

'Nnnn . . . NO!'

It was the first word that I'd ever heard her say.

'No?' I laughed. 'You don't like my reading, eh?'

'N-n-n-n-no,' she repeated again. 'No. No.'

Her voice was croaky and quiet but it was wonderful to hear her speak.

'Well, in that case, I'd better put the book away then,' I told her.

Over the next few days, Louisa tried to say more and more. She wasn't speaking in full sentences by any means and sometimes she struggled to form the sounds but she could soon say 'hi', 'no' and 'go'. She had enough words to be able to boss me and the nurses around.

A few days later, Mr Edwards asked to see Brian and me at the hospital.

'I wanted to chat to you both about Louisa,' he said. 'I feel that she's made enough progress so that we can start to think about moving her out of ICU and onto a neurological rehab ward.'

I had been nervous about the meeting as I wasn't sure what he wanted to talk to us about so to hear this was such a relief.

'Oh wow,' I sighed. 'That's amazing news.'

'There's still a long way to go in terms of rehab,' he warned us. 'But from a medical point of view, she's always been breathing on her own, her vitals are good, and her fractures and the other injuries she sustained in the crash are healing nicely.'

He informed us that a scan had showed that the swelling on her brain had gone down.

'Basically what I'm saying is that we feel she's out of immediate danger and it's more about rehab now rather than intensive care.'

'But she's still bed-bound and tube-fed,' said Brian.

'Yes, and all that can continue on the ward,' agreed Mr Edwards. 'But things can start in terms of physio and speech therapy with the eventual aim of getting her back on her feet. She'll still be monitored closely but she's progressed significantly and doesn't need intensive care any more.'

'That's wonderful,' I said.

'How do you think she's doing in terms of damage to her brain?' asked Brian.

'She's definitely out of what we would describe as a coma and she's regained a good level of consciousness,' Mr Edwards told us. 'As with all of this, when it comes to the brain, it's impossible to predict. I would hope that she keeps on progressing to a point where she can eat and dress herself and be mobile again, but it's going to be a long, slow process.'

He explained that after nearly eight weeks in a hospital bed, Louisa was probably going to have to relearn to do most of those things again.

'But she's young and her brain is showing a great capacity to heal.'

'Thanks for all your help, Mr Edwards,' I told him. 'We really appreciate all the kindness and compassion that you've shown to Louisa.'

'She's a very lucky girl,' he replied. 'Things could have been very different.'

After saying goodbye to Brian, I went to see Louisa in ICU.

'I've got some very good news,' I told her. 'Mr Edwards thinks that you're well enough to transfer to a ward. That's really positive, Louisa,' I said, grasping her hand. 'You're doing so well and you're only going to get better. Everything's going to be OK.'

Her mouth was moving and I could tell she was trying to say something to me.

'W-www-w' she mouthed.

'It's OK,' I said. 'Take your time.'

'Wa-wa,' she continued. 'W-where . . .'

'Where!' I said. 'That's amazing. Where . . .?'

'Mmm-mmm,' she struggled. 'Mmmm.'

I could see she was really trying but it was so hard for her to form the sounds. Tears of frustration filled her eyes.

'Don't worry,' I reassured her. 'Don't get upset. The words will come soon.'

'Mmmm . . .' she continued. 'Mu-mu-mu. Wh-wheree mmm-mum-mummy?' she repeated as her lips started to form the words.

I looked at her and my heart started to race. It had been the question that I'd been dreading for the past two months.

Where's my Mummy?

I felt panic surging through my body. I owed Louisa the truth but I was her foster carer and not her social worker and therefore it wasn't my job to share this information. I knew it would be unethical and get me into a lot of trouble if I told her the truth now without consulting Brian first.

She repeated it again.

'Where's your mummy?' I asked and Louisa blinked twice. She hadn't mastered saying 'yes' yet.

'When I leave here, I'll definitely go and find out for you,' I said to her.

In the heat of the moment, it was all I could think of to say. I wasn't lying to her but I wasn't telling her the full truth either. I knew that before we told her, I needed to talk it through with Brian and come up with a proper plan and this would buy me some more time.

As soon as I got home that afternoon, I called Brian and told him what had happened.

'I was so unprepared,' I told him. 'I honestly didn't know what to say to her.'

'You did the right thing, Maggie,' he replied.

We both agreed that she needed people around her when she was told so I made it clear to Brian that I wanted to be there.

'The thought of it makes me sick but I think I should be there,' I added.

'I agree,' he nodded. 'Normally, as Louisa's social worker, it's my responsibility to tell her. But in a way, Maggie, you're the person who is the most familiar to her. You've been the one by her side since her early days in hospital.'

I could see where this conversation was going and I wasn't sure that I liked it.

'So, I was thinking,' Brian continued, 'how would you feel about being the one to tell her? I would be there of course, but I do feel in these circumstances, it would be better coming from you.'

It was certainly something that I didn't want to do. In fact, even the thought of it made my stomach churn. But I agreed with Brian. It probably was better coming from me.

A shiver ran through my body as I thought about what on earth I was going to say. A young girl's life was about to be torn apart and I was the one who had to do it.

EIGHT

The Truth Hurts

This was it. The moment I'd been dreading for the past couple of months, ever since the first day that I'd met Louisa. We were about to destroy her whole world and I felt sick to my stomach.

Brian and I gathered by her bedside in the ICU. I could tell Brian was nervous too as his balding head was shiny with perspiration and he kept patting it with a hankie.

It was Louisa's last few days there before she was moved to a rehab ward. Brian hadn't seen her for a couple of weeks so he reminded her who he was and chatted to her. She looked at him with a slightly confused look on her face, unaware that it would soon become apparent to her why she had been appointed a social worker.

After a little while, Brian gave me a meaningful glance as if to signify that the time was right to deliver our news.

I cleared my throat and prepared to break Louisa's heart.

'Louisa, Brian and I wanted to talk to you about why you're in the hospital,' I began. 'Do you remember what happened? Do you know how you got injured?'

Louisa looked confused.

'Nnn-n-n-o,' she said, shaking her head.

I forced myself to continue on, even though every fibre of my being was wishing that I didn't have to do this. I made sure that I spoke slowly and clearly so that hopefully Louisa was able to take in as much of it as possible.

'What I'm about to tell you is going to be very difficult for you to hear and it might be hard for you to understand at first,' I explained. 'A few weeks ago, you and your parents went to collect your new puppy, Luna.'

'Luna!' she grinned. 'Luna!'

'Do you remember Luna?' asked Brian, and Louisa nodded.

'On the way back from collecting Luna, your car was in a very bad crash,' I told her. 'You were very seriously injured, which is why you've been in hospital these past two months.'

I explained how she had hurt her head badly, broken her leg and had lots of cuts and bruises. As I spoke, Louisa was looking straight at me but she showed no reaction and I couldn't tell what she was thinking.

'You've been very poorly but the good news is, the doctors think you're through the worst of it now,' I smiled. 'Mr Edwards is really pleased with all of the progress that you've shown.'

I paused and took a deep breath. Brian gave me a supportive smile.

'But I'm afraid I've got some really, really sad news to tell you . . .'

Instinctively, I reached over and held Louisa's hand.

'Unfortunately your parents, Simon and Karen, didn't survive,' I said, desperately trying to stop my voice from trembling with emotion. 'I'm so sorry to tell you this, Louisa, but your mum and dad both died in the crash.'

I couldn't be ambiguous about it or try to soften the blow. I had to tell it as it was so there was no room for confusion.

Louisa stared blankly at me, a dazed expression on her face.

'Do you understand what Maggie is telling you?' Brian asked her. 'We know this must be so hard for you to hear but we felt that you needed to know the truth.'

Louisa remained expressionless.

'I'm so sorry, flower,' I told her gently. 'Even though your parents are not here any more, I want you to know that you're not on your own. You're safe and when you feel better and you're ready to come out of hospital, I will look after you. You can come back to my house and hopefully, in time, it will become your home too.'

I felt tears welling up in my own eyes as both the relief and the enormity of the situation hit me. I just wanted to weep for this poor girl and everything that she had been through and the pain and the hurt that she had to come. I couldn't imagine how devastating it must be to be told that you were an orphan at thirteen. The two people she loved most in this world were dead.

We both looked at Louisa, waiting for a reaction.

She stared at us blankly for a moment then she burst out laughing. It wasn't just the giggles, it was hysterical laughter, as if someone had told her the funniest joke that she'd ever heard.

Brian and I looked at each other in complete bemusement. This certainly wasn't the reaction either of us had been expecting. I'd prepared myself for her to scream and shout and be angry or to cry hysterical tears. But laughter? That was completely bizarre.

'Louisa, do you understand what we're telling you?' I asked her. 'Your parents died in the car crash.'

She nodded her head.

'D-dd-dead,' she sniggered. 'Dead. Dead. Dead.'

Then she burst out laughing again.

'Luna?' she asked.

'Where's Luna?' asked Brian and she nodded.

'I'm so sorry but I'm afraid Luna died in the crash too,' I told her.

I thought hearing about the puppy might be the thing that helped her understand and accept what had happened but she just giggled to herself.

We sat with Louisa a little while longer, but neither Brian nor I said anything more about her parents. To be honest, I didn't know what to say as I didn't know whether she had understood the information and taken it in.

'Well, that didn't go the way I'd expected it to,' said Brian as we walked down the corridor of the ward together.

'Let's see how things go over the next few days,' he told me. 'It might be that she has a delayed reaction. It's probably not properly hit her yet.'

I knew he was right. It was an awful lot for her damaged brain to process.

As I wandered down the ward back to Louisa's room, Claire, the senior charge nurse, was at the nurses' station.

'Everything OK, Maggie?' she asked. 'You look a bit down.'

I went over to talk to her as I felt the nursing staff needed to know what had just happened.

'We've just told Louisa about her parents,' I said.

'Gosh, I'm sorry that must have been so hard,' sighed Claire. 'How did she take it?'

'Unbelievably, she laughed,' I shrugged. 'That wasn't at all what I was expecting and it's floored me a bit.'

Suddenly, much to my surprise, I felt tears prick my eyes.

'Sorry, I don't know why I'm getting emotional,' I sighed, embarrassed. 'It was just so unexpected, that's all.'

I'd got myself so wound up about telling her and then to get that reaction, it just made me wonder whether we had done the right thing. Maybe we'd expected too much, too soon, and her understanding wasn't there yet?

'I'm sorry, Maggie,' nodded Claire. 'It's worth knowing that when someone has a brain injury then it can completely change the way they express themselves. If it makes you feel any better, I've had patients who often show inappropriate emotions. They lose that ability to react to something how we normally would expect them to but hopefully it will get better over time.'

'I know,' I sighed. 'It's not Louisa's fault.'

'At least you've told her now and if she has any questions, we know what to say,' said Claire.

I felt so sad about it all and how confusing it must be for Louisa, who probably had no concept of social workers and foster carers. All we could hope was that somehow, deep down inside, she had taken in the information and could start to process it.

By the time I was heading to the hospital the next morning, I'd pulled myself together.

'Maybe I'll try to talk to her about her parents again?' I thought to myself as I walked down the ward. I stopped at the door to Louisa's room and did a double take. The whole room had been cleared out. The bed was empty and the monitors lay unplugged and silent.

'Hey Maggie,' said a voice.

It was Wendy, one of the nurses.

'Where is she?' I gasped.

'They've moved her to the rehab ward,' she told me. 'They came down early this morning. Sorry, did you not realise it was today?'

'No,' I said, shaken.

It felt strange walking away from ICU and back through the hospital. The rehab ward was at the other end of the building and it took me a while to find it.

I was worried it would be too much for Louisa after the eery quiet of the Intensive Care Unit but, much to my relief, it was a small ward with only six beds. I headed to the nurses' station, aware that there was a whole new team of staff to get to know.

I explained who I was to a young blonde nurse.

'Well, you haven't got far to go,' she told me, signalling to a bay with the curtains pulled round it. 'She's right here.'

She gently pulled back the curtain and I peered through. Louisa was lying in bed, fast asleep.

'She's pretty much been like that since they brought her down,' she told me. 'Change can be a huge thing especially when you're coming from the ICU, so I think she's exhausted.'

It was strange to see her on a ward rather than in her own private room. They had moved her things with her but all her personal belongings were in a cardboard box next to her bed.

She still had the feeding tube down her nose but it was lovely to see her without all of the other tubes and wires and not to have the endless beeping of monitors. For the very first time, she was wearing her own pyjamas rather than a hospital gown and suddenly she looked like a normal hospital patient rather than someone fighting for their life. It really did feel like progress.

While Louisa slept, I decided to sort through her things. I stuck some of the photos of her and her friends to the side of the cupboard next to her bed like I'd done in her room in the ICU. I put the faux sunflowers in their vase on top as well as the framed family photo and the one of her parents on their wedding day and placed her teddy and the Jellycat bunny next to them. Then I went to introduce myself to the staff.

As always, they were extremely busy, but I wanted them to know a little bit about Louisa, what had happened to her and who I was.

The nurse in charge of the ward that day was a male nurse called Johnny.

'Don't worry, Maggie, we'll keep you updated,' he told me.

They obviously had all of Louisa's notes and medical history.

He described how the first priority was for her to start having sessions with a speech and language therapist.

'The SLT can help to make sure Louisa can control her lips, tongue and jaw, which she'll need for both speech and swallowing,' he explained.

Mr Edwards had already explained to us that having a brain injury was a bit like being a baby. Louisa was going to have to learn to do everything again, from eating and talking to sitting up and walking.

Unusually, Louisa slept the whole time I was there that morning.

'Try not to worry,' Johnny reassured me. 'Change is a huge thing for brain injury patients and she's probably exhausted. We'll call you if there are any problems.'

As I drove home, I felt that I had abandoned Louisa. It was a relief when I went in the next day and found her sitting up in bed for the first time.

'Wow, look at you,' I grinned. 'It must be nice to be able to sit up and look around.'

Louisa still looked dazed and confused but she gave me a weak smile.

I chatted away to her as I always did.

'While you were asleep yesterday, I unpacked your stuff,' I told her.

Now she was properly upright, she could see things a lot better. I pointed out the photos of her friends from school.

'That's you with Becky, Phoenix and Frankie,' I told her. 'Frankie has been to see you in hospital a couple of times.'

Louisa stared blankly at the photos and showed no reaction and I wondered if she recognised them.

Then she pointed to the framed photo on the top of the cupboard.

'Those are your parents,' I told her.

Louisa studied it.

'W-www,' she mumbled. 'W-where?'

My heart sank when I realised what she was asking. Clearly she hadn't taken in anything that we'd told her the previous day and I was going to have to break her heart.

'Can you remember Brian and I talking to you about this yesterday, Louisa?'

She shook her head.

All I could do was be honest and tell it as it was.

'You had a very bad car crash,' I told her. 'You were seriously injured and unfortunately your mum and dad died.'

This time there was no laughing; there was just a blank, expressionless face staring off into the distance.

'Louisa, do you understand me?' I asked her. 'Your parents didn't survive the crash and they died. I'm so sorry but we're all here to help you and look after you.'

Louisa looked straight at me.

'No,' she said matter-of-factly. 'No, no, no!' she shouted as she shook her head.

I just didn't know what she was thinking. Over the next couple of days, she didn't say any more about her parents.

Then the following morning I arrived at the ward and Johnny asked if he could grab me for a chat.

'Louisa had a very restless night,' he told me. 'She seemed very agitated and she wouldn't sleep.'

'That doesn't sound like her,' I said, concerned, as she normally slept for hours each day.

When I walked into Louisa's bay, she was curled up in bed. I realised that clutched in her arms was the photograph of her parents.

'Hi Louisa,' I said gently. 'How are you doing?'

She looked up at me with wide, bloodshot eyes and pointed at the photograph.

'Gone,' she shouted angrily. 'Gone, gone, gone.'

That's when I knew that she finally understood the terrible truth.

NINE

Celebration and Acceptance

Life on the new ward was much busier for Louisa. The aim was to get her into a predictable routine so she knew what was happening each day. It was a balancing act as it was important that she didn't become overtired.

Speech therapy had started and her speech was really coming along. She could form words more easily now and she'd started to speak in short sentences. I could see that she still sometimes struggled to find the right word or work out what she wanted to say and we couldn't have a proper conversation yet, but we were slowly getting there.

'I think she finally understands about her parents,' I told Brian, when he called for a quick update one morning.

I told him what had happened with the photo.

'She looked upset and she said the word "gone",' I said. 'I think that means she understands that they're dead.'

'I hope you're right,' he replied. 'That feels like a big step.'

It was a massive relief to know that Louisa could at least start to try to come to terms with what had happened.

I quickly got to know the staff on the new ward as I spent several hours there each day. They were as understaffed and stretched as the team in ICU but they were equally as dedicated and caring. Whenever they could, they tried to make time for a quick chat or an update on Louisa. From the charge nurses to the cleaners and Louisa's lovely cheerful physios, Helen and Julie, everyone was very welcoming.

I was walking down the ward one afternoon, when Julie pulled me to one side.

'Maggie, I thought I'd better mention to you that Louisa was asking me about her parents.'

'What about them?' I said.

My heart sank when I heard her reply.

'She was asking me when they were coming to see her.'

All my hopes that Louisa had finally taken in what we'd told her were suddenly destroyed.

'She was getting quite agitated about it,' she told me.

'I'll go and have a word with her,' I sighed.

When I pulled back the curtain to her bed, Louisa was holding the photograph of her and her parents in her hand.

'When . . . are . . . coming?' she mumbled when she saw me. 'See me?'

I felt so wretched having to deliver the same terrible news. All I could do was keep things clear and simple until she eventually got the message.

'You were in a car accident, Louisa,' I told her. 'You were very badly injured and that's why you're here in the hospital.'

She nodded.

'I'm so sorry to tell you this, Louisa, but your parents didn't survive the crash and they died.'

I couldn't make it any more straightforward than that.

Louisa looked at me with shocked, sad eyes.

'Dead?' she repeated and I nodded.

It was like we were stuck in the cruellest version of Groundhog Day.

I still didn't know if there was any understanding there or if she would be asking the same question in another few days.

I sought some advice from Louisa's new consultant, Dr White, when Brian and I met her for the first time later that week.

'We're really struggling with her remembering that her parents have died,' Brian explained. 'She seems on the face of it to accept that there was an accident and that she's been in hospital, but even though we tell her that her parents didn't survive, she will ask about them again a few days later.'

'Every brain injury is different,' Dr White told us. 'There's no set pattern to what a patient will or won't remember. We often find that with brain injuries, the long-term memory works better than the short-term. I've got patients who can't remember what they've just eaten or the sentence they've just spoken but they will clearly remember something that happened over a decade ago.'

I told her that some time ago Louisa had remembered the name of the new puppy they had collected on the morning of the crash.

'Do you think she will remember the crash itself?' asked Brian.

We hadn't actually asked her that question yet. She had only just started putting words together so I wasn't sure if she could cope with such a traumatic conversation or express herself to that extent.

'There are no guarantees but I think it's highly likely that she won't remember what happened,' Dr White told us. 'Generally most neurological patients I see don't remember how they sustained their injury.'

The brain was such a complicated organ and no one seemed to know anything for sure.

'Even though Louisa doesn't remember us telling her that her parents have died, she does seem to know who they are,' I said. 'She's able to recognise them from the photographs that she has next to her bed.'

'It's still very early days in terms of a brain injury,' Dr White reassured us.

'But what can we do?' I sighed. 'I feel like we're emotionally torturing her having to tell her this horrendous thing several times over.'

Dr White reassured us that we were doing all the right things.

'Just keep repeating it in a very factual way and hopefully Louisa will start to learn and remember. Whatever you talk to her about, use simple language,' she said. 'Try not to bombard her with too much information. Simple instructions and conversations are best. If you're asking her questions, make sure they're ones she can answer with a yes or no. I think anything else could be too overwhelming at this stage.'

'Thank you,' I said. 'That's all really helpful.'

'Her recovery is going to be inconsistent so prepare yourself,' she told us. 'This is all new and exhausting for her. My advice would be to celebrate the good days and accept the bad.'

One thing Dr White suggested was that seeing familiar faces might help so I was pleased when I got a call from Frankie's mum, Margaret.

'Frankie keeps asking about Louisa and I wondered how she was doing,' she told me.

I explained what had been happening and how Louisa had been moved out of the ICU and onto a ward.

'In fact, if Frankie wants to visit her, I think it would be a really good time,' I replied. 'Her speech is really coming on so she can communicate a little bit more now and she's sitting up and most of the tubes and wires have gone. It might be really helpful for her to see a familiar face.'

We arranged for Frankie to visit a few days later after school.

As Dr White had advised us, I was being careful not to bombard Louisa with too much information all at once. I knew her brain was struggling to process things so I didn't mention that Frankie was coming until she arrived.

Margaret gave me a call when they got to the hospital.

'You've got a visitor,' I told her. 'Your friend Frankie is coming to see you. I'm just going to go and get her.'

Louisa stared at me blankly.

I went to meet Frankie and Margaret by the entrance to the ward. Visitor numbers were limited to two people so we couldn't all go at once to see Louisa.

'I can stay with Frankie if you want while you go and get a coffee?' I suggested.

'OK,' said Margaret. 'Give me a call when she's finished.'

I'd already warned them both that it wouldn't be a long visit as I knew Louisa could only cope with five or ten minutes at the most.

'She looks a lot more like the old Louisa – all those bleeping machines are gone and she's sitting up,' I told Frankie as we walked through the ward. 'She won't be able to have a long chat with you but she can say the odd word and hopefully understand what you're saying to her.'

'That's brilliant,' she smiled.

When we got to Louisa's bay, I pulled back the curtains. She was sitting up in bed.

'Look who's come to see you,' I told her.

Frankie grinned.

'Why don't you sit down, flower,' I said, pointing to the chair by Louisa's bed.

'Hi, Lou Lou,' she said shyly. 'How are you feeling?'

Louisa just stared at her, a blank look on her face.

'I bought you some nail varnish in your favourite colour,' she told her, showing her a little bottle of bright blue polish. 'And some lip balm that smells like cherries.'

'Oh that's lovely,' I smiled. 'Louisa, now you're out of intensive care I can ask the staff if it's okay to paint your nails.'

Up until now, Louisa hadn't said a word. She was just sitting there, staring at Frankie.

'Who are you?' she asked suddenly.

Frankie laughed.

'What do you mean silly?' she giggled. 'You know who I am!'

Suddenly, alarm bells started ringing and I jumped in to try to salvage the situation. But it was too late.

'Louisa, this is Frankie. Your friend from school. She came to see you when you were in the Intensive Care Unit.'

Louisa frowned.

'No,' she said suddenly, turning her head away from her. 'Don't know you.'

Frankie looked horrified.

'You remember me don't you, Lou Lou?' she said, close to tears.

'No,' replied Louisa, shaking her head. 'Go! Bitch!' she shouted.

She swiped the bottle of nail varnish Frankie had brought her off the bed. It cracked as it hit the floor leaving blue splashes of polish everywhere.

Louisa was angry and Frankie was distressed, so I quickly ushered her out of the cubicle and back onto the ward.

'I'm so sorry, lovey,' I told her. 'I didn't know Louisa was going to react like that. I thought it would do her good to see a familiar face and someone she knew before the crash.'

I could have kicked myself for getting it so wrong. Naively I hadn't even thought about the possibility that Louisa might not remember her.

I quickly called Margaret to explain what had happened and we all went to the canteen together.

'I'm so sorry for putting you in that position, Frankie,' I told her.

I felt awful as I could see she was upset.

'That's not what she was like before,' she sobbed. 'Louisa would never be that mean. She's supposed to be my best friend.'

'Sometimes when people have been in a coma, their brain gets all muddled and it takes a long time to repair itself,' I explained to her. 'Louisa's not quite herself yet and there are some things that she's struggling to remember. I know her short-term memory is affected so I was hoping that her long-term would be better.'

'Do you think she'll ever remember me?' asked Frankie sadly.

'No one knows for sure,' I told her. 'But hopefully as her brain heals then she will. She's not the old Louisa at the moment.'

The sad fact was, I didn't know whether she would be the old Louisa ever again. After a traumatic brain injury, I was becoming all too aware that some people were changed permanently.

I felt a lot more useful these days as there were lots of things that I could do when I went to visit Louisa, whether it was helping her with some of the exercises the physios had given her or teaching her how to eat.

Helen, Louisa's physio, was working on her grip so she was doing lots of exercises where she was squeezing putty and balls in her hands. She also got a triangular bar dangling down above her bed that they were aiming to get her to pull herself up on.

'We're trying to build up her upper body strength,' she told me.

One morning I was there when Helen was trying to get Louisa to sit on the side of the bed.

'We want to eventually try to get you to stand up and put weight on your feet again,' Helen told her. 'We need to wake those legs up as you haven't been using them for the past three months.'

Scans had shown that the break in her left leg had pretty much healed.

As she pulled the sheet down and attempted to swing her legs around, Louisa shook her head.

'Come on,' said Helen gently. 'Let's get you sitting up on the side of the bed.'

Louisa shook her head.

'No!' she said. 'Can't.'

'Yes, you can – trust me,' encouraged Helen. 'I'm going to count to three then I'm going to swing your legs gently around and pull you so you're sitting at the side of the bed with your feet on the floor. One, two . . .'

'No!' shouted Louisa, pushing her away. 'Don't want to. Fuck off.'

'Louisa!' I gasped. 'I'm so sorry, Helen.'

'That's OK,' she replied. 'I've been working with patients with brain injuries for years and being sworn at comes with the job. I'm used to it.'

The girl in front of me seemed so far away from the sweet, kind Louisa that everyone who had known her was telling me about.

'I think that's enough for today,' Helen told her. 'But you're not getting off that easily, Louisa. We're going to try again tomorrow.'

Louisa shook her head firmly and scowled at her.

I walked Helen out of the cubicle.

'I'm sorry she was so rude to you,' I told her. 'I think she's finding it hard.'

'I don't think she likes me very much today,' she replied. 'But that's OK, rehab is tough and it's normal to get angry and frustrated.'

She explained how Louisa needed to keep repeating the same movements.

'The more she rehearses it, the easier it will get,' she told me. 'We're retraining her brain to remember the movements. We need to get her sitting and then standing and then, once she's built her strength and muscle tone back up, walking hopefully.'

'That seems such a long way off at the moment,' I sighed.

'It is,' nodded Helen. 'Her body is very weak, but she's young and she's strong, and I'm hopeful that she can do it.'

However, there was still one question that was weighing heavily on my mind.

'Is there a chance that she might never walk again?' I asked her.

I knew there was a possibility that Louisa had progressed as far as she was ever going to and she would be left in a wheelchair or permanently disabled.

'If I'm being completely honest, there is,' sighed Helen. 'She might never walk again or she might walk with a stick or a limp, but she might relearn everything and be running marathons in ten years. That's the problem with brain injuries, it's the unknown.'

I was getting used to hearing this a lot recently.

Teaching Louisa how to eat again was also a slow process. It was like having a baby again and it was hard for me to believe that it was only been a few months ago that I had been weaning Micah onto solids.

Doctors had left Louisa's feeding tube in until she was eating enough to sustain her. The first time I tried to feed her, I think I was more nervous than I'd ever been with any baby.

'We need to get her used to sucking and swallowing again,' the nurses had advised me.

Like a baby, we were starting her off on fruit purées. She needed to learn to cope with different textures and temperatures.

'Yum, this one's apple,' I smiled as I held out a plastic spoon for Louisa to try.

But she turned her head away.

'Don't want it,' she spat.

'Louisa, have a little taste,' I smiled. 'It's really nice.'

She shook her head.

'Don't want it,' she repeated, louder this time. 'Go away!'

'Louisa, please,' I begged her. 'We want to get rid of the feeding tube and we can't do that until you learn to eat again. I know it's frustrating but you can do it.'

Louisa looked at me with sad eyes. I did sympathise with her. Every day must seem like an endless list of impossible tasks for her.

'Please give it a try,' I said gently. 'I'm begging you. Let's at least try to get rid of the feeding tube.'

Louisa opened her mouth like a baby bird and stuck her tongue out. I held out the spoon and she licked a bit off the top of it.

'Good girl, I said. 'Do you like it?'

Before she could reply, she started coughing furiously.

Oh my goodness, she was choking.

Panicking, I quickly reached over and pressed the nurses' bell. Thankfully, a few seconds later, Johnny, the charge nurse, came running. Louisa was still coughing violently.

'Please help her,' I begged him. 'I gave her some puréed apple and I think she's choking,'

He quickly raised the back of the bed up so Louisa was sitting upright, then held a beaker of water to her lips.

'Here sweetheart,' he said. 'Have a little sip of this if you can.'

It was such a relief when I saw her take a tiny gulp of water. Finally the coughing stopped.

'She's certainly keeping you on your toes,' he said as he saw my weary expression.

'She is,' I sighed.

'It's going to be a bit like this at first because she has to learn the swallow reflex again,' he said. 'Coughing is a good sign because it shows that she knows how to clear her throat. You're doing great, aren't you Louisa?'

Every day there was a new challenge for her and I could see why it was exhausting. It was like she'd been reborn and she had to learn how to walk, talk and go to the toilet again. It certainly was a rollercoaster.

TEN

Mistaken Identity

The man sitting in front of me looked eerily like Louisa's dad, Simon. He had identical dark hair that I'd seen in the photographs and the same piercing blue eyes that Louisa had inherited.

'I'm so sorry about your brother,' I told Martin. 'From what I've seen from photographs, you two look like twins.'

'A lot of people used to say that when we were growing up,' he smiled sadly.

Martin had arrived from Australia a few days ago and Brian, Louisa's social worker, wanted us all to meet up to talk about Louisa.

'How is Louisa doing?' he asked. 'Poor girl, seems like she's really been through it.'

'She has,' I nodded.

'She's very lucky to be alive,' agreed Brian.

Although I didn't think 'lucky' was something Louisa felt at the moment.

'Would you like to go and visit her in the hospital?' Brian asked him.

'Definitely,' Martin nodded. 'I know she doesn't know me and we've never met before but I'm the only family she's got left now. I'd like to see her for my brother's sake.'

We also talked about the funeral. Martin had started making arrangements with a funeral director and he'd set a date in ten days' time.

'I hadn't seen my brother in years and I'd only met Karen a few times so I'd love to get Louisa's input on the things they might want,' he said. 'Even if it's just songs that they liked or happy memories that she has of them.'

'What do you think, Maggie?' Brian asked me.

'I'm happy for you to visit Louisa but I honestly don't think she's up to helping you with funeral arrangements,' I shrugged. 'I wish she was because I think it's good for children to get involved but her brain is still very muddled after the crash. We're still not 100 per cent sure that Louisa even understands that her parents have died.'

'Gosh, that's so sad,' sighed Martin.

I explained to him that her communication was limited.

'She can still only say a few words,' I said. 'And she gets very angry and frustrated and her understanding isn't great so I don't think it's something that she could help you with.'

'What do you think about her going to the actual funeral itself?' asked Brian.

This was something that I'd been thinking about a lot in the past few days. I was normally a big advocate of children going to funerals. I believed death should be talked about openly with them and they should have a chance to say goodbye to their loved one as often it helped to give them some sort of closure. But, in Louisa's case, I wasn't so sure.

'Will it even be physically possible for her to be there?' Martin asked. 'Or is she still too badly injured?'

'Maggie, what do you think?' replied Brian.

Louisa hadn't left the hospital in the three months since the crash, but she was off all of the monitors now and she was stable and I was sure there were ways to work round her catheter and feeding tube. She would need to use a wheelchair and I knew that getting dressed and going out after so many months in a sterile hospital was going to be a huge deal for her.

'I think we'd need to ask her consultant and get her permission first,' I said. 'It would be a lot for her to cope with both physically and mentally so I'd want to make sure that we could do it safely.'

'If she doesn't understand, do you think there's any point in her being there?' asked Martin.

I explained to him about brain injuries and how it was the complete unknown.

'The hard part is, no one can tell us when Louisa will recover and if she's even going to recover,' I told him. 'Every bit of progress that she makes is a blessing.'

'But I do think we should try to get Louisa to the funeral,' I added. 'I think it's important to give her the opportunity to say goodbye to her parents.'

Even if she didn't understand it completely, I was sure there would be a small part of her that took it in. I didn't want her to look back months or years later when hopefully she was further down the road of recovery and feel regret, or blame others for not giving her the chance to be there.

'I'll talk to Louisa about what she wants,' I said. 'She might refuse to go and if so, we have to respect that.'

Her mood was extremely temperamental at the moment. Her body and brain were not working properly and it was going to take a long time for both of them to heal. Every day was confusing and exhausting for her and I could feel her frustration.

'Will you tell Louisa that I'm coming to see her?' asked Martin.

'I will,' I told him. 'But her short-term memory isn't great at present so there's no point really until just before you arrive.'

I'd learnt the hard way from Frankie's visit that Louisa might not act the way we wanted her to, so I made sure that I warned Martin.

'I honestly don't know how she's going to be with you,' I told him. 'So please be prepared for the fact that you might not get the warmest of welcomes.'

'I understand,' he nodded 'All I can do is try.'

As we all walked out together, I could see there was something else that Martin wanted to say.

'Maggie, thanks for agreeing to take Louisa on,' he said. 'I felt bad saying no but I have my own life in Australia and I have nothing in common with a thirteen-year-old girl who I've never met before.'

'I understand,' I replied. 'You had to make a decision that's right for you.'

We arranged for Martin to come to the hospital the following day. I'd suggested that he visited first thing in the morning when Louisa was less likely to be tired but he had an appointment with the funeral directors. When Brian called to let me know they were on their way, it was nearly lunchtime. Louisa had just finished a session with her other physio, Julie.

'How did that go?' I asked Julie on her way out.

'She did so well,' she smiled. 'Her strength is coming on and she really worked hard today.'

I got Louisa a beaker of water and told her the news.

'Louisa, your Uncle Martin is coming to see you this morning,' I told her.

She looked confused.

'Don't know him,' she said, shaking her head.

'You won't remember him, lovey,' I explained. 'He lives a very long way away in Australia and you've never met him before.'

I told her how he was her dad's younger brother.

'He hadn't seen your dad for a long time but he wanted to come and see you. Is that OK?'

She shrugged ambivalently.

'I'm just going to meet him and your social worker Brian and then we'll be back to say hello. OK?'

Louisa nodded.

I walked out to the front of the hospital but it was another fifteen minutes before I saw Brian and Martin in the distance heading towards me.

'I'm so sorry,' puffed Brian. 'It took me ages to find a parking space.'

'No problem,' I said.

'I told Louisa that you were coming and she seemed fine with that,' I said, turning to a nervous-looking Martin.

I led them through the hospital to Louisa's ward. But when I gently pulled back the curtain to her bay, she was fast asleep.

'Oh bless her, she's nodded off,' I sighed. 'She gets very tired after physio and she still sleeps a lot in the day.'

'I could come back later?' suggested Martin.

'Oh, it's OK,' I said. 'I'll get us all a cup of tea and I'm sure she'll eventually wake up.'

I got us all a burning hot polystyrene cup of tea from the vending machine and Brian pulled up some chairs for us next to Louisa's bed. After chatting for five minutes, I noticed her eyes starting to flutter.

'Here she is,' I smiled.

'Hi flower, did you have a nice sleep?'

'Hello Louisa,' Martin smiled.

Louisa's eyes opened and when she finally focused on Martin, she did a double take. Her face dropped.

'Daddy!' she gasped. 'Dad!'

Martin looked at Brian and I in a panic.

'No, no, lovey, this isn't your dad,' I said quickly. 'It's your uncle. Remember I told you about your Uncle Martin who was coming to see you from Australia?'

I could tell by the confused look on Louisa's face that she'd clearly forgotten.

As she stared at Martin with the same blue eyes as her dad's, she looked like she had seen a ghost.

'Dad?' she asked again.

'Hi Louisa,' he said nervously. 'I'm your Uncle Martin although people tell me I do look a lot like your dad. It's lovely to meet you.'

'Daddy?' she gulped.

'No Louisa, this isn't your dad,' I said firmly. 'This is your dad's brother. Remember your dad died in the car crash? I know they look very alike but this is your Uncle Martin.'

Louisa stared at him with a confused look on her face while Martin shifted uncomfortably in his seat.

'I'm so sorry about your mum and dad,' he told her. 'Simon and I were really close growing up and even though I hadn't seen him for a long time, I'll miss him.'

I could see Louisa desperately trying to process what was happening here.

As the realisation hit, she burst into tears.

'Go!' she told him, curling up in a ball and sobbing. 'Go away!'

'I'm so sorry,' mumbled Martin. 'I didn't mean to upset you.'

'Go away!' she screamed.

Martin got up and left, quickly followed by Brian and I.

'I'm so sorry about that,' I told him. 'It's why I wanted to warn you – it's difficult to predict how she's going to respond. She's all over the place at the moment.'

'It's OK,' he replied. 'She's been through a lot. It just makes me wonder whether her going to the funeral is the right thing.'

Ultimately, as Louisa's social worker, it was Brian's decision.

'I need to have a think about it,' he told us. 'Maggie, if you could talk to the medical staff about it and see whether it's even possible, that would be great and then I can have a follow-up chat with them.'

'I will do,' I replied.

Martin said he would keep in touch.

'I'm actually over here in the UK for eight weeks,' he told me. 'One thing I need to do after the funeral is clear out the family home.'

The landlord was waiting to put it back on the rental market.

'I would love Louisa to be able to sort through some of her things and take what she wants but I'm not sure if she's up to that.'

'We'll see,' I told him. 'We have to take things day by day at the moment.'

We had the funeral to get through first.

After I had walked them out, I went back to the ward to find Louisa had fallen back to sleep.

One of the nurses had brought her some soup for lunch, which she put on the side.

'I think I'll let her sleep,' she smiled. 'Poor love looks exhausted.'

To be honest, so was I. I never knew how Louisa was going to react from one minute to the next.

I knew the first step was to speak to Louisa's medical team about whether they thought it would be possible for her to go to the funeral.

I broached the subject with the charge nurse, Johnny, when I visited the next day.

'I think it's something that you need to discuss with her consultant,' he told me. 'If she's happy then we'll do everything we can to try to make it happen.'

Dr White arranged to see me that afternoon in her office. I explained that it was her parents' funeral.

'To be honest with you, Maggie, this isn't something that we would normally do with a patient like Louisa,' she told me. 'But they are her parents and these are extenuating circumstances, which is why I am willing to consider it.'

'Thank you,' I replied. 'If there's a way that we could make it happen then I do think it could help Louisa accept that they're gone and consolidate that in her mind. What do you think?'

'I think it will be a lot for her,' sighed Dr White. 'She's still incredibly weak although she's stable and is improving. I think it would very much depend on how she is on the day, and if there are any concerns at all from the medical staff then she won't be able to go.'

'I understand,' I said. 'Her health has to come first.'

I knew it was going to take a lot of planning.

'I think even if she does go, then it should be for as short a time as possible,' she told me. 'And I will see if the ward can spare a member of staff to go with you. We wouldn't normally do this but, as you say, it might help Louisa's understanding if she gets to say a proper goodbye to her parents.'

'Thank you,' I told her. 'I really appreciate you helping us out with this.'

I called Brian and told him what the consultant had said.

'I think we should try and get her there,' he said. 'Even if it's just for half an hour of the service.'

Funerals were such an important part of the grieving process and I was convinced that even just seeing their coffins would help make it more real for Louisa.

'I agree,' I said. 'Although it sounds like we're not going to know for sure until we see how she is on the day.'

Now all we had to do was talk to Louisa herself about it.

'I think, keep it as simple as you can,' my supervising social worker, Anna, told me when I asked for her advice about it. 'What would you do if it was a younger child?'

'I'd talk to them about it and perhaps read them some story books about funerals,' I replied.

'I think you need to do the same with Louisa,' she told me. 'She might not understand or even remember, but small parts of it might sink in.'

'You're right,' I said.

As Dr White had advised us, it was best to keep things very simple and factual.

I had a couple of picture books that I'd used in the past with very young children to explain about funerals so I brought them to the hospital. Sadly I'd had several children who had lost their biological grandparents while they had lived with me, including one little six-year-old boy whom I had fostered when his birth mother was having problems with depression. Tragically, she had taken her own life and books like this had helped enormously to prepare him for the things that were going to happen after she had died.

If I talked to Louisa about it every day then hopefully she would start to understand.

'Louisa, I've been talking to your consultant about you going to your mum and dad's funeral,' I told her. 'A funeral is a chance to say goodbye to your mum and dad.'

'Gone?' asked Louisa.

'Yes, that's right, flower,' I told her. 'They've gone. They died in the car crash and you were injured.'

Louisa nodded.

'When someone dies, it's good to be able to say goodbye to them and think of all the happy times that you have had with them. Would you like to say goodbye?'

Louisa nodded.

'See them?' she asked.

'No, you won't see them,' I told her.

I explained as simply and as clearly as I could how their bodies would be there in the chapel in coffins and then they would be buried in the ground. I didn't know whether she had ever been to a funeral before and, even if she had, whether she remembered it.

'It will be very sad as I know you loved them very much but it will be good for you to have the chance to say goodbye.'

'Sad,' nodded Louisa.

I knew I'd said enough about it for now. Louisa could only process a small amount of information at a time so I didn't want to overwhelm her.

The following day, I brought it up again and showed her one of the picture books.

'This is a book all about funerals,' I explained. 'I thought we could read it together before we have your mum and dad's funeral next week.'

'Mum?' asked Louisa hopefully. 'Where is Mummy?'

I took a deep breath and calmly explained.

'Remember there was a car crash and your parents died?' I said. 'You were badly hurt and that's why you're in hospital.'

'Gone?' said Louisa.

'Yes,' I nodded. 'They're gone. They died, Louisa.'

Sometimes it felt relentless. I was learning that the brain was such a strange thing. Sometimes Louisa seemed to remember what had happened, and other times the information had completely gone.

'This is what happens at a funeral,' I told her gently, opening the storybook and showing her some of the pictures.

It was designed for very young children but I hoped that, somehow, it would help her to understand.

'A funeral is a chance to say goodbye to someone that we love,' I said. 'We'll go to the chapel and your parents' coffins will be there at the front. People might sing songs and be sad but we can remember all of the happy times you had with them.'

'Happy?' smiled Louisa and I nodded.

'It will be a sad day too but I will be there with you,' I told her. 'And Brian your social worker and your Uncle Martin.'

Louisa looked puzzled.

'Don't know him,' she said, shaking her head.

As the doctors kept reminding me, each injury was unique and every person recovered differently. I felt dreadfully sorry for Louisa and what she must be going through.

I was trying to prepare her as best I could but I didn't even know if she would actually make the funeral. Would she get the chance to say goodbye? And, if she did, would it help?

ELEVEN

Saying Goodbye

Over the next few days, I gently reminded Louisa about the funeral. I didn't want to bombard her with information but I tried to mention it briefly each time I saw her, just to try to help it to sink in.

In the background, plans were being put in place. Staff on the ward had organised for a nurse to come with us. I knew how stretched they were so I really appreciated how much they were going above and beyond to try to make this happen for Louisa. They'd also arranged for us to borrow a wheelchair and I had booked an accessible taxi to take us to and from the chapel at the cemetery.

All of this was dependent on Louisa's health on the day.

'Any sign of a temperature, a cough or an infection, anything at all, and I'm afraid I won't be able to authorise her to leave the hospital,' Dr White warned me. 'Her body is still weak and I'm not prepared to take any chances.'

'I understand,' I replied.

I didn't want to put Louisa's health at risk either, but both

Brian and I felt it was important to at least try to get her there so she had a sense of saying goodbye to her parents.

The good news was that Louisa was now eating enough so that the doctors felt she was getting adequate nutrition, enough to be able to remove her feeding tube. She was also strong enough to be able to sit up most of the time in bed. It was all real progress.

Brian called me a few days before the funeral to talk through the arrangements. It felt like a huge military operation getting her out of the hospital for the first time in nearly four months and to the chapel and back, and I think we were both nervous about it and desperate for it to go smoothly.

'Have you thought about what Louisa's going to wear?' he asked me.

I knew getting her up and out of bed and to the service was going to be exhausting enough without having to get her dressed as well.

'I'm going to keep her in clean pyjamas and I've bought her a smart black coat to go over the top,' I explained. 'She'll have a blanket over her bottom half so no one will see what she's wearing.'

The medical staff had stressed the importance of keeping her warm. It was late spring but Louisa was used to the high temperature of the hospital ward and she had lost a lot of muscle tone so I was worried that she would feel the cold.

As Louisa could sit up for longer periods now, it meant the nurses could transfer her into a plastic bath chair and take her for a shower. She could stay sitting in the chair while they washed her down. For nearly four months, she'd only had bed baths and her hair had been washed in a bowl with jugs of water at the end of her bed.

The day before the funeral, they took her for her first shower.

'You'll feel so much better for having a proper wash,' I told her.

When they wheeled her back, it was lovely to see her long dark hair freshly washed and wet around her shoulders.

'You're going to look so smart,' I told her as I gently combed it through for her. 'Your parents would be so proud of you.'

It was perfectly poker straight just like her mum's was in the photos next to her bed. My heart was heavy with sadness when I thought about what Louisa was going to face tomorrow. I would look at her confused face and wonder whether she even understood. Were we doing the right thing in trying to get her there? I could see how even something as simple as having a shower had completely tired her out.

'Your hair looks lovely,' I told her as I put the comb down on the side. 'I'll see you tomorrow, flower.'

'Remember it's the funeral,' I told her gently.

She looked puzzled.

'Remember we're going to say goodbye to your mum and dad?'

'Dead,' she said, matter-of-factly.

'Yes, you're right lovey,' I nodded. 'I'm afraid they are dead. They died in the car crash and tomorrow is your chance to say goodbye.'

I knew it might sound brutal to an outside observer but over the past few weeks, I'd trained myself to say things in a very straightforward, simple way in the hope that Louisa would understand them. Some days I felt she understood everything and others I didn't have a clue what she was thinking.

As I drove home that afternoon, my stomach was churning with dread.

I called Anna for a pep talk when I got back.

'Are we doing the right thing, forcing her to go to the funeral?' I asked her.

'Maggie, you're not forcing her,' she told me. 'You and Brian have made an informed decision. Your job as a foster carer is to act in the child's best interests and that's exactly what you're doing. You know the importance of funerals and children being able to say their goodbyes. This way, Louisa will have no regrets as you gave her that opportunity.'

I knew she was right, but it would be a lot easier and less stressful not to take her.

'But what if something happens?' I asked her.

'Nothing will happen,' Anna sighed. 'You've got a nurse with you and the doctors have given you their approval.'

Despite her reassurances, I hardly slept that night for all the worrying.

The service was at 11 a.m., so by 9 a.m., I was pulling up at the hospital, buzzing with anticipation at what felt like the huge task ahead of me.

'How is she?' I asked the charge nurse, Johnny, as I walked into the ward.

'She seems fine,' he said. 'She had a settled night and she's eaten some breakfast. We've given her a quick check over and she seems well. I think you're good to go.'

To be honest, I wasn't sure if that was a good or a bad thing.

'Go now?' asked Louisa when she saw me.

She had obviously understood that something was happening.

'Yes', I told her. 'Today we're going to leave the hospital for a little while and go to the chapel for your mum and dad's funeral.'

She nodded.

I'd given us plenty of time so that we could take things slowly. I gave Louisa a wash and helped her to brush her teeth. The nurse who was coming with us was called Sally and she came to introduce herself.

'I'm just going to go and get the wheelchair,' she told me.

I brushed Louisa's hair and gently got her coat on for her. I'd brought her some thick woollen socks and a pair of trainers that I'd taken from her house all those months ago. It must have felt odd as she hadn't had shoes on her feet for months.

'Right, I think we're ready to go,' I said nervously when Sally came back with the chair.

Sally and another nurse lifted Louisa into the wheelchair and I tucked a thick blanket over her legs. I talked her through everything before it happened.

'We're going to go outside now,' I said.

Louisa looked around in awe as Sally wheeled her out of the ward and through the main hospital. I noticed her flinch as the sliding doors of the hospital opened and she felt the wind on her face.

'It must feel strange after so many months inside,' I told her.

She didn't say anything.

Louisa was very quiet in the taxi. She looked out of the window with big blinking eyes. The world must have felt so strange, bright and noisy after the stuffy, quiet atmosphere of the hospital.

I couldn't help but worry about her. Every time we turned a corner or went over a pothole or speed bump, I looked at her nervously, worried about the impact it could have on her frail body.

'Are you OK, lovey? I asked her. 'Do you need a sip of water?

'It's a bit bumpy on these roads, isn't it?'

'I think she's doing just fine,' smiled Sally.

We'd arranged with Martin to get to the chapel just before the service started as I didn't think it would do Louisa any good to be waiting around for a long time. As we got closer, I could see there were cars parked all down the road leading up to the cemetery.

'Wow,' I sighed. 'It looks like there are a lot of people here.'

My heart sank when I saw the two empty hearses outside the chapel, reminding me once again why we were here. Martin and Brian were standing outside waiting.

'I'll quickly go and have a chat to your uncle and Brian,' I told Louisa. 'You stay with Sally.'

Brain smiled when he saw me.

'How's Louisa doing?' he asked.

'She's extremely quiet but we made it,' I replied. 'It looks like a good turnout.'

'Yes,' nodded Martin. 'The chapel is packed. I honestly didn't know what to expect as I didn't know any of my brother's or Karen's friends or who to tell about the arrangements. But word obviously got out.'

He described how there were people there from Simon's work as well as lots of Karen's hairdressing clients and friends.

'Louisa's teacher Miss Grey is here and some of her friends from school and their parents,' he told me.

'Oh, that's lovely of them to come,' I said.

Brian explained that the church staff had opened the side door of the chapel so we could take Louisa in that way.

'It saves her having to be pushed through the centre of the church past everyone,' he said. 'It might be less intimidating for her.'

None of us were sure how she was going to react.

'After the service we'll come straight out into the cemetery and have the burial,' Martin told us.

'We'll just have to see how we go and how Louisa is,' I told him.

Afterwards he had arranged to have a wake in a local pub but I had already ruled that out as being too much for Louisa to cope with on top of everything else.

'Right, the service is due to start in a minute so I'd better go in,' said Martin.

'We'll take Louisa in now,' I told him.

The driver lowered the ramp down at the side of the cab and Sally gently wheeled Louisa out.

'Let's get you sitting up a bit better, sweetheart,' she told her, hoisting her up so she was sitting more upright in her chair, then she tucked the blanket in around her legs. I was suddenly feeling very nervous so I was glad Sally was there for help and reassurance.

'Right, let's do this,' I said.

Brian and I led the way through the side door and into the chapel while Sally pushed Louisa behind us.

The place was full and I felt all eyes on us as we made our way to the front pew that Martin had kept free for us. Sally went in first, followed by Brian, and I sat at the end next to Louisa's wheelchair. I looked around and noticed Frankie and her mum Margaret. I caught Miss Grey's eye and she gave me a sympathetic smile.

'Are you OK, flower?' I whispered to Louisa, adjusting the blanket so that it was snug around her legs.

She'd hardly said a word up to this point. She was staring at the front of the chapel with huge, startled eyes. I suddenly realised what she was looking at.

To the right of us, at the top of the church, side by side, were two wooden coffins with gleaming brass handles. On top of each one were matching floral tributes. Spelled out in white and purple flowers one said 'Mummy' and the other said 'Daddy'.

The tragedy of what had happened hit me all over again. Two lives lost and a little girl left all alone. A whole family destroyed forever. It was unbelievably sad.

I reached over and held onto Louisa's frail hand.

'It's going to be OK,' I whispered to her. 'I'm here. You're OK.'

She didn't say a word, her blue eyes staying firmly fixed on the coffins of her parents. Familiar doubts crept into my mind. Was this the right thing to do? Was it helping her to understand what had happened?

I'd read the children's picture book about funerals so many times to her over the past week. But had it really sunk in what was happening here?

Suddenly the organ started playing and the congregation stood up.

I could see the noise had startled Louisa as she jumped in her wheelchair.

'No!' she shouted. 'Don't like it!'

'Shhh, it's OK,' I soothed, patting her hand.

The vicar started the service but to be honest, I wasn't listening to what he was saying; I was focused on Louisa. I looked across at Martin, who was dabbing his eyes with a handkerchief.

'And now we're going to play one of Karen and Simon's favourite songs,' I heard the vicar say.

People started sobbing as Queen's *Days of Our Lives* came blaring out of the speakers at the front of the church.

Louisa yelped and put her hands over her ears.

'No!' she shouted, rocking backwards and forwards in her wheelchair. 'Stop!'

'It's OK,' I said, trying my best to calm her. 'It's just the music.'

'Don't like it!' she shouted. 'Stop it! Stop it!'

People were looking over at us as Louisa whimpered and rocked back and forth. I shot Brian a panicked glance.

'I think we need to take her out,' Sally whispered to me.

I knew she was right. I could see that it was all too overwhelming for her – the people, the noise, the crying, the music.

We quickly shuffled out of the pew and Brian opened the side door and we wheeled Louisa out.

I breathed a sigh of relief as the fresh air hit my face.

Louisa was still whimpering. I put my arms around her.

'It's OK,' I told her, stroking her hair. 'You're OK.'

'Don't like it,' she whimpered and I could see she was crying.

'I know you don't,' I replied. 'We're going to take you back to the hospital now.'

Sally got Louisa some water while Brian and I had a chat.

'Was it worth traumatising her for?' I sighed.

We'd only been there for fifteen minutes.

'At least we tried, Maggie,' he replied. 'She saw her parents' coffins and she might have taken some of it in. Hopefully it will help her at some point in the future to start processing her grief.'

I wasn't so sure.

'I'll stay on for the rest of the service and let Martin know what happened,' Brian told me.

'Thank you,' I said. 'I think we just need to get Louisa back.'

I could see from the way she was slumped in the wheelchair that she was absolutely exhausted. It had all been too much for her.

She slept all the way back in the taxi. I knew sleep was a great healer and it would help her brain to process the events of the day. Maybe some of it would sink in? Perhaps it was best that she wasn't there to see her parents' coffins being lowered into their graves.

'Poor love,' sighed Sally. 'It's just all so tragic.'

'It really is,' I agreed.

Louisa remained asleep even when we wheeled her down the ramp out of the taxi and back through the busy hospital.

'How did it go?' asked Johnny as we took her back into the ward.

'It was very sad,' I sighed. 'It was all too much for Louisa to cope with in the end, but we tried.'

Sally and I took her back to her bed. I knew we would have to wake her to take her coat off and get her back into bed.

'She could probably do with having a drink and eating some lunch,' Sally advised and I knew she was right.

I gently shook Louisa awake. She looked so disorientated.

'We're back at the hospital, flower,' I told her gently. 'Let's get this coat off you and get you back into bed.'

Sally went off to find her some lunch.

'Mum?' she asked as I took her trainers and socks off. 'Dad?'

'We went to their funeral today,' I told her. 'They died and it was very sad.'

'Coffins,' she said firmly. 'Flowers.'

'Yes, that's right,' I nodded. 'Their bodies were in the coffins and Martin got them some beautiful flowers from you to put on their graves. It was good that you could say goodbye,' I told her.

'Goodbye,' she repeated. 'Gone.'

'Yes, they've gone lovey,' I said. 'It's very sad and I'm so sorry.'

Suddenly a tear rolled down Louisa's cheek.

'Gone,' she said again.

It was as if she was trying to get it straight and make sense of it in her muddled mind.

'Where I go?' she asked suddenly.

'When you get better and you leave the hospital, you will come and live with me,' I told her. 'I will look after you at my house.'

Suddenly an angry look flashed across Louisa's face.

'No!' she said. 'Don't like it! Go to *my* house.'

I wasn't prepared for this sudden outburst. How did I explain that her house didn't exist any more? Next week her Uncle Martin was going to be clearing it out and strangers would be moving in.

The only home that she had now was with me. I got her settled into bed and smoothed down her hair.

'No,' she told me angrily, pushing me away. 'Bitch!'

I was shocked by this sudden anger, but I couldn't blame her. Today had pushed Louisa to her limits and her broken brain and body simply couldn't cope.

TWELVE

Standing Tall

Louisa's face grimaced in concentration. Her physios, Helen and Julie, stood on either side of her, each gripping onto one of her arms.

'OK, Louisa,' said Julie. 'Are you ready? After three, we're going to pull you up onto your feet.'

I held my breath.

'One . . . two . . .' said Helen.

'No!' Louisa shouted, shaking her head. 'No! Can't do it!'

'Yes, you can,' Helen told her calmly. 'We'll both be holding onto you and I promise you that we won't let you fall. And if you feel comfortable, you can lean on the standing frame for support.'

'No!' she said firmly, wriggling free of their arms. 'Don't want to! Go away!'

It was a fortnight after the funeral and Louisa was really finding her voice but not yet her feet. Her speech was coming along brilliantly. She still spoke slowly but she could put full sentences together now and express herself well. Although sometimes that was a curse as well as a blessing.

I did feel for her though. Rehab was hard and exhausting and I understood her frustration at having to learn how to do every little task again. Her progress was slow but she could sit on the edge of the bed now and today Helen and Julie were trying to get her to stand up and put weight on her feet for the first time.

'Louisa, it's just for a few seconds,' Julie reassured her. 'I know it's tiring and it's scary but I promise you, we've got you.'

'Come on, Louisa,' encouraged Helen. 'Let's give it a go. You can do this.'

'Fuck off bitch!' she spat suddenly.

'Louisa!' I gasped, shocked. 'Please don't speak to Helen like that.'

'Don't worry,' said Helen. 'I know Louisa's just feeling frustrated. Come on,' she told her. 'Shall we try this?'

'Don't want to,' sighed Louisa, folding her arms. 'Not doing it.'

She kicked the standing frame over and it clattered to the floor.

'Go away!' she snapped.

I went and sat next to her on the bed.

'Louisa, nobody is going to make you do this but it's about helping you to build up your strength so you can leave the hospital,' I told her calmly. 'You've got to do this to get better.'

'Don't want to,' she repeated. 'Bitch.'

Ignoring her bad language, I took a deep breath and tried to stay calm.

'Helen and Julie have got other patients to see who need their help,' I told her. 'So they're going to go now and hopefully when they come back tomorrow you'll be willing to give standing up another try.'

'I won't!' she shouted. 'You can't make me do it!'

Then suddenly, much to my astonishment, she turned to me and shoved me off the bed.

Thud.

I winced as my bottom slammed onto the hard hospital floor.

For someone who had been in a coma for months, Louisa had quite a lot of strength in those sinewy arms.

'Ow,' I yelped, rubbing my coccyx.

'Are you OK, Maggie?' asked Helen, concerned.

Louisa stared at the wall and didn't say a word.

'I'll live,' I sighed. 'Although I think I'm going to have a whopper of a bruise there by tonight.'

She and Julie helped me up.

'Why are you helping her?' Louisa snapped. 'You should be helping me. I'm the one doing all the work.'

'We're all trying to help you, Louisa, but you have to let us,' said Helen firmly. 'We'll see you tomorrow and hopefully you will feel better then.'

Louisa just scowled and looked away.

I hobbled down the ward with them so we could have a chat.

'I'm sorry about today,' I told them. 'She's having a lot of these angry outbursts lately.'

'It's OK,' said Julie. 'I think you bore the brunt of it.'

'Do you think I should say anything to Louisa?' I asked them.

It was unacceptable behaviour and, even after everything she'd been through, I couldn't just let it slide, could I?

'As I've told you before, Maggie, we're used to working with patients with brain injuries,' said Helen. 'You wouldn't believe the number of times we've been sworn at or hit and kicked. You've got to remember, it's not their fault. Their brain is damaged and sometimes you've got to pick your battles. Louisa will hopefully get better.'

'Do you think she *can* get to a place where she can learn to walk again?' I asked them.

'Once she gets over the dizziness and she builds up the muscles in her legs, I really think she can do it,' said Helen.

I felt like the baddy but sometimes I had to be hard on Louisa. It was painful and difficult but she needed to do it if she wanted to keep progressing.

The angry outbursts did worry me and I had a chat with Dr White about it, who could only repeat what she'd told me previously.

'I'm afraid mood swings and this kind of aggressive behaviour are common with patients who've had a traumatic brain injury,' she said. 'Louisa's frustrated, she still gets very tired and her mind is still struggling to process and deal with the real world. She can't control it but I know it doesn't make it any easier for you to cope with.'

'How should I handle it?' I asked her.

'Try to stay calm and don't react,' she replied. 'Help her to calm down and maybe try and redirect her to something else. Hopefully these mood swings and temper outbursts will ease over time.'

'Is there a risk that they won't?' I asked. 'Could her personality have changed and this is what she's like now?'

'Yes, it could be,' she told me honestly. 'There are no guarantees. Sometimes that area of the brain, which enables us to manage our emotions, is permanently damaged. All we can do is hope that it isn't.'

*

Brian called me one afternoon.

'Martin's started clearing out the house,' he told me. 'He wondered if we could take Louisa there so she can decide what she wants to keep.'

'Honestly I think it will be too much for her,' I told him.

After what had happened at the funeral, I knew the whole process of getting her ready to leave the hospital, getting her to the house and back again would be exhausting for her.

'Her emotions are so up and down as well,' I told him. 'Plus she physically wouldn't be able to get up and down the stairs. Why don't I meet Martin there and help him to go through some stuff?' I suggested.

'If you don't mind, Maggie, that would be great,' he said. 'I think he's really struggling.'

I knew it was a lot for Louisa to take on board but now she was more coherent, I wanted to try to explain what was happening so she felt more included.

I broached the subject when I went to visit one morning.

'Your Uncle Martin has to clear out your house and he wondered if there was anything that you wanted him to save for you,' I asked her gently.

'Why?' she gasped. 'Why's he clearing our house?'

'Because no one's living there any more, flower, and he has to give the keys back to the letting agent so they can rent it to someone else,' I explained.

Louisa looked puzzled.

'But that's *our* house,' she sighed.

'I know it's hard, but Martin wondered if there was anything that belonged to your mum and dad that's special to you and you wanted to keep?'

'But what about my room?' she asked. 'I want my things.'

'I'm going to pack everything in your bedroom so don't worry about that,' I told her.

'But why are you packing it?' she asked. 'I want to go back and live there.'

'I know you do,' I told her. 'But I'm afraid that you can't. Your mum and dad are not there any more, Louisa. They died and the house needs to be rented out to someone else.

'But you're not on your own,' I reassured her. 'You're going to come back and live with me at my house and I will look after you.'

Louisa looked furious.

'Well, I don't want to,' she snapped.

'I'm afraid you don't have much choice, lovey,' I told her.

It was a hard thing to tell a child but I had to be honest with her.

I didn't want to upset her any more so I didn't mention it again and hoped that she would have time to process it.

A few days later, I pulled up outside the terraced house again. I thought about how much had changed since I'd first met that PC there all those months ago. It already felt like a lifetime ago. Louisa had progressed so much but she was still in hospital.

I knocked on the door and an exhausted-looking Martin let me in. As I walked into the living room, I could see it was in disarray. The cupboards were open, there was stuff spilling out all over the floor and there was a mountain of cardboard boxes piled up in the middle of the room.

'How's it going?' I asked him.

'There's so much to sort through,' he sighed. 'But I'm slowly getting there.'

'What are you going to do with it all?' I added.

'I'm trying to save a few personal items but, to be honest, most of it's probably going to end up going to a charity shop or a house clearance company. It's tragic really,' he sighed. 'My brother and Karen's whole life is in this house and I'm just getting rid of it.'

'What else can you do?' I sympathised.

It was sad seeing this once-happy home completely torn apart like the family who had lived in it.

'Do you know if there's anything Louisa might want to keep?' he asked me.

'I did ask her but I don't think she really knows,' I told him.

I was going to have to try and make that decision for her.

'It would be great to have three or four items of well-worn clothes from Simon or Karen as I'd like to get them made into memory bears for Louisa.'

'What sort of clothes?' he asked.

'Perhaps some of Simon's shirts or jumpers or pyjamas, a top or a dress from Karen. Something patterned or distinctive so Louisa will recognise the fabric. Even jeans could work.'

'I don't think Simon was really the shirt-wearing type,' Martin smiled. 'But I'll bear that in mind when I'm sorting through their clothes to send to the charity shop.'

I told him that I would clear Louisa's bedroom.

'I'm going to box all of her things up and then when she gets to my house, she can sort through it and decide what she does and doesn't want to keep,' I said.

Rather than unpack it all for her, I was keen to give her some element of control.

'What do you think she would want to keep from the rest of the house?' he asked.

'It's so hard to know what would be sentimental to her,' I sighed. 'I don't know if Karen had any jewellery but if you could save some of that for her, that might be nice.'

'Do you think she wants any of the furniture or Karen's hairdressing equipment?' asked Simon.

'I don't have the room for any of that sort of stuff, I'm afraid,' I said.

It was so hard to guess what items would mean the most to her and what she would want to remember her parents by. I thought about what I would want to save if there was a fire at my house.

'If you could keep any photographs either in frames or albums and any jewellery, that would be great and I can show them to Louisa,' I told him.

The house was full of knick-knacks but nothing that I thought a thirteen-year-old girl would be interested in and there weren't many books or pictures on the walls.

'You can have a look round if you want and take anything that you think Louisa might like,' Martin suggested.

It felt sad and wrong picking through the pieces of someone's life. I was a stranger to her parents and it felt like I would be invading their privacy by going through their cupboards and drawers.

'It's OK, I'm happy for you to decide,' I replied. 'You knew them better than me. I'll concentrate on Louisa's room.'

I spent the next few hours packing up the rest of Louisa's things. I'd been in so much of a hurry the last time I was here,

I hadn't really looked at her bedroom properly. Like the rooms downstairs, it was as if it had been frozen in time. It broke my heart to think about the final morning that she was here, probably rushing out of the door to pick up their new puppy. Her laundry basket was full of dirty clothes still waiting to be washed and there was a half-drunk glass of water on the side. And now everything was covered in a thick layer of dust.

I had to put my feelings to one side and get on with the job. It was a typical teenager's bedroom and there was stuff everywhere. The wardrobe and drawers were bursting at the seams and there was more stuff shoved under the bed.

Even though I'd taken a few basics and quite a few of her clothes the last time I was here, there was still lots to sort through. I packed up CDs, magazines, school books, make-up – all the things I knew were really important to a teenage girl – into cardboard boxes. I didn't envy Martin having to sort through the whole house.

After three hours, I was exhausted but it was done. Louisa's room was pretty much cleared except for the furniture.

'Have you got a vacuum and I can give it a once-over?' I asked Martin.

'Don't worry, I've got cleaners coming in to give it a deep clean before I give the keys back to the letting agency,' he said.

Martin helped me carry the boxes to my car and handed me another couple that were filled with photographs and albums.

'Right then,' I said. 'Thanks for all of your help.'

'Oh Maggie, there's something I need to give you before you go,' said Martin. 'One second.'

He ran into the house and came back out clutching a clear plastic bag. He handed it to me and I could see that inside there was a large silver watch and three rings – two gold bands and a single diamond solitaire.

'The police gave them to me,' he said. 'It's the jewellery Karen and Simon were wearing on the day of the crash. I thought Louisa might want them, especially their wedding rings.'

It felt strange looking in the bag and thinking that these items were still here but their owners weren't. Through the plastic, I shuddered as I noticed that the watch had dried blood on the strap.

I must remember to wipe that off before I show it to Louisa, I reminded myself.

'I'll make sure I give them to Louisa,' I told him, putting them carefully into my handbag. 'I'm sure she'll treasure them.'

Martin explained that he was in the UK for another couple of weeks before he had to go back to Australia.

'If you want to visit Louisa at the hospital before you go back, let me know,' I told him. 'It would be nice for her to see you again.'

After all, he was the only member of her family left.

The next day, I went to visit Louisa as usual and I took a couple of the photo albums that Martin had saved for her. I had a flick through them the previous night and they were lovely, happy family pictures – caravan holidays, Christmas days, birthday parties; Louisa growing up through the years and her smiling parents always by her side. I knew that no family was perfect but I could see the warmth in the photos – the look of pride on Simon's face as he posed with his daughter and the love in Karen's eyes as she sat with Louisa on her lap at the beach.

Louisa's long-term memory so far seemed better than her short-term and Dr White said it would be helpful for her to look at old photographs and talk about things that had happened in the past so I was keen to show them to her.

'Look what your uncle Martin saved for you from the house,' I told her, handing her one of the albums.

She opened it up and her face broke out into a huge grin.

'Oh I know that place!' she gasped. 'That's my nan's caravan in Wales. We always used to go there for our holidays except for last year when we went to Spain.'

She flicked through a few more pages.

'Oh and that's my birthday party when I was eight,' she laughed. 'We went bowling and Dad was rubbish.'

Suddenly the expression on her face changed. It was as if a cloud had passed over the sun.

Louisa closed the album with a bang and pushed it away from her.

'I don't want to look at these any more,' she said.

'That's OK, flower,' I told her. 'I'll keep them safe for you at my house so when you come home, you can look at them anytime you want.'

A look of anger flashed across her face.

'I want to go back to my house, not yours,' she spat.

'I know you do,' I told her. 'I understand that it's so hard for you but it's not your house any more.'

'It's not fair,' she told me. 'I wish you were dead and not my mum.'

They were hurtful words but I completely understood why she was saying them.

'I know, lovey, and I understand why you feel that way,' I said. 'None of this is fair and I'm so sorry that this is happening to you.'

The impact of the last few months was finally hitting her. Louisa was realising that she had lost everything – her home and her parents, and I realised that she must feel very alone.

I went to take the album to put it in my bag. But, before I could, Louisa picked it up and threw it off the bed.

'Go away,' she said. 'I hate you.'

I knew the next few months were going to be a rollercoaster as Louisa struggled to come to terms with things.

A couple of days later, I headed to the hospital to find Louisa in the middle of a physio session with Helen and Julie. She was sitting on the edge of her bed.

'Maggie!' smiled Julie. 'Just in time. Louisa's got a surprise for you.'

'Ooh that sounds intriguing,' I grinned.

'Take a seat,' said Helen, pointing to the plastic chair in the corner.

I did as I was told and sat down.

'One, two, three . . .' said Julie.

I watched as she and Helen winched a nervous-looking Louisa onto her feet. I could see the determination on her face and her legs were shaking with the effort but she'd done it.

'Louisa, you're standing up!' I cheered. 'That's incredible. You've done it!'

'Are you OK?' Helen asked her. 'Not too dizzy?'

Louisa shook her head. I could see that it was taking all of her effort and concentration to stay upright.

'OK, when I say "go" you're going to let go of me and Julie and use the walking frame to lean on instead. OK?'

Louisa nodded again.

'Go!' said Helen.

I watched nervously as Louisa gripped the walking frame with one shaking hand then the other. Helen and Julie stood to one side.

'Look at that!' smiled Julie. 'You've done it – you're standing all on your own!'

'Well done, flower, that's such an achievement,' I said.

After a coma and five months in a hospital bed, she was finally standing on her own two feet, something we all feared she would never be able to do.

'Enough!' wailed Louisa suddenly. 'I've had enough!'

'It's OK, we're here,' Julie told her.

Julie and Helen quickly moved the walking frame, took an arm each and gently lowered her back down onto the bed.

It had taken every ounce of energy that she had and I could see that she was exhausted.

'That was amazing,' I told her. 'I'm so, so proud of you.'

'It was brilliant,' said Helen. 'I told you you could do it. Every day we'll practise and we'll get you standing for longer and longer, then it will be time to get you walking.'

'Walking?' gasped Louisa.

'Yes,' laughed Helen. 'We're not going to stop there. We'll have you running marathons by the end of the year, just you wait and see.'

After all the doubts and unknowns about what Louisa would understand and be able to achieve, the fact that she was able to stand felt like a ray of hope. And we had to cling onto that and hope that things were finally going to get better at last.

THIRTEEN

Homewood Bound

It was time for another LAC (Looked After Child) meeting to assess where we were. Brian, Anna and I had come to Social Services along with Miss Grey, Louisa's head of year eight at her secondary school, and also a hospital social worker called Maria. (Most hospitals have their own social workers and their job is to help make sure that patients have somewhere safe to go when they're discharged from the hospital.)

'Is Martin not coming?' I asked as I looked around the room.

'He emailed the other day to say that he was flying back to Melbourne,' said Brian.

'Oh,' I replied, surprised and slightly disappointed. 'I thought he might have come to the hospital to see Louisa before he left.'

'I got the sense that he was glad to be going home,' sighed Brian. 'He's had a lot to sort out over the past eight weeks.'

He went on to tell us that the family home had now been cleared and the agents had already re-let it. As Martin had power of attorney, he'd sorted out most of the admin and what was left he was going to organise from Australia.

'It's sad that he didn't want to try to forge some sort of relationship with Louisa for her sake,' I sighed.

'People are strange, Maggie,' nodded Anna. 'But then again, I can understand why a forty-something man might find it difficult to relate to a teenage girl.'

While I could understand why Martin didn't feel that he could take Louisa on full time, I was annoyed that he hadn't visited her at the hospital again. He was the only family member she had left in the world, except for her elderly grandma, and it would have been nice for him to at least try to have a relationship with her or offered for her to visit him one day when she was older.

'Well, Louisa is doing well by the sounds of it,' said Brian.

He explained that he'd had an email from Helen updating him on her physio sessions.

'Yes,' I replied. 'In the last few weeks, we've made lots of progress.'

I described how she could now stand with the help of a frame and how the aim now was to build up the muscles in her legs so that she could learn to walk again.

'That's brilliant, Maggie,' smiled Anna. 'She's come such a long way.'

'What about her speech?' asked Brian.

He generally went to the hospital every two or three weeks to visit her.

'I know the last time I saw her she was a lot more coherent and we could almost have a normal conversation,' he added.

'Yes, that's really come on too,' I told him. 'She's doing her sessions every other day with the speech therapist.'

'From the doctor's initial worries that she might be permanently brain-damaged or vegetative, it sounds like she's starting to make progress,' added Brian.

'She really is,' I said. 'I know there were so many unknowns but she's come such a long way since the crash.'

After nearly half a year in hospital, at last we were starting to look at the prospect of Louisa finally being discharged.

'Louisa will soon be back on her feet and hopefully walking so I think we need to start putting plans in place for her to go and live at Maggie's house,' said Brian.

Maria, the hospital social worker, nodded in agreement.

'From the hospital's point of view, once she's mobile then we feel she is ready for discharge,' she told us. 'From a medical perspective, she doesn't need any continuing care and her speech therapy and physio can all be continued in a domestic setting.'

The first step was to get an occupational therapist to visit and do an assessment of what equipment Louisa would need. Social Services had a number of OTs that worked with them.

'The main issue is the stairs,' I said, thinking of the steep narrow staircase in my house.

'Hopefully the hospital wouldn't look at discharging her until she's walking a few steps and can cope with the stairs?' Brian asked Maria.

'I can make a note that she will need to be moderately mobile,' she nodded.

There wasn't enough room for a stairlift, plus I knew the cost was exorbitant and I wanted to try to avoid having to have a hospital bed downstairs. I wanted Louisa to come back when she was at a point where she could have her own bedroom and get up and down the stairs with my assistance. I could see how frustrated she became with having to be reliant on nurses and medical staff in the hospital and I wanted her to feel like she had some level of independence and control before she came to live with me.

'Even when she's discharged, she's going to need a lot of help,' warned Maria. 'Things like showering, toileting, getting around.'

'That's OK,' I smiled. 'I'm able to do all of that.'

I'd cared for children before who needed that level of help. Lots of older children came into the care system who sadly didn't have the skills to wash themselves and keep themselves clean so I was happy to teach Louisa.

In a way, it was going to be nice to feel useful again. The past six months had been strange as I didn't feel as if I was truly fostering Louisa. I was visiting her in the hospital for hours but I'd go home at night to an empty house and it felt odd, like I wasn't doing a proper job. I hadn't been able to take any other placements on because even though Louisa wasn't living with me, by the time I'd driven to the hospital and spent several hours with her and then driven home again and written up my notes, it didn't leave much time for anything else. I was also very tired.

I knew that once she was discharged, it was going to be full-on. 'It's going to be a huge adjustment for Louisa after so long in hospital,' said Maria. 'She's not used to the real world and it's going to be overwhelming and exhausting for her at first.'

I'd seen it in children that I'd fostered in the past. When they'd been in hospital for months, they tended to get institutionalised. Everyday sounds like a kettle boiling or a washing machine could really freak them out and they weren't used to doing anything for themselves.

'It's going to take a lot of adjusting for everyone,' agreed Brian.

He suggested that we start some settling in sessions like we did when a child like Micah was being adopted.

'We could organise an OT to bring Louisa from the hospital to Maggie's house,' he said. 'It could just be for a short time at first – just half an hour or so. She could see the house and familiarise herself with it and get used to being away from the hospital.'

I knew it was also a case of her familiarising herself with me too. Even though I visited her at the hospital for hours every day, we had never lived with each other.

'When she comes to visit, she would have to stay downstairs at first,' I said. 'Until she can master getting up and down stairs safely.'

I described how, so far, she had reacted badly to the idea of coming to live at my house so these visits were going to be important.

'She still hasn't accepted that her family home has gone,' I said.

'I can understand why it doesn't seem real to her,' sighed Anna. 'The poor girl's woken up from a coma to find her whole life in pieces.'

None of us would ever fully comprehend what that must feel like and it was no wonder that she was struggling to accept it.

'We also need to talk about school,' added Brian. 'Miss Grey has kindly come along today.'

'I'm so happy to hear that Louisa's on the mend,' she smiled. 'We're happy to have her back any time.'

I knew there was a long way to go in terms of her schooling. As well as walking and talking, she would have to learn how to read and write again although the doctors had told us she might have retained some knowledge.

'I think now that her understanding is better, she can start sessions with a tutor at the hospital,' said Brian.

Most hospitals provided some form of education on their paediatric wards for children who were in hospital long-term; in fact, many of them had their own school room.

'The ideal scenario is to get her back into learning as soon as possible,' said Brian. 'But I think mainstream school is a long-term goal.'

'She's going to be very tired at first,' I nodded. 'She's recovering well but she still gets very confused and muddled, especially with her short-term memory.'

'We're here when she's ready,' smiled Miss Grey. 'We could look at putting her on a reduced timetable at first or only doing a couple of days a week. We're happy to work with you to make it achievable for Louisa.'

Although she'd progressed so much, going back to school seemed a long way off in the future. I knew that before the crash, she'd been very academic but I wondered how her brain injury was going to affect her learning in the long-term.

'Does anyone have any other concerns or anything else they want to raise?' asked Brian.

'Maggie?' said Anna, prompting me.

I hated to say anything as Louisa had been through so much and was progressing so well but my one big worry was her mood swings.

'She's very up and down,' I sighed. 'She shouts and swears sometimes and she's lashed out a few times.'

'We see this a lot in patients with brain injuries,' nodded Maria. 'Sometimes it improves, sometimes it doesn't. They can get very angry.'

'Her understanding and awareness is much better but she's still very tired and she struggles to process things, which I think leads to the frustration,' I said. 'I have spoken to the consultant about it and she said there are no guarantees but hopefully it should improve over time.'

I knew that Anna and I would have more discussions between ourselves if my concerns continued.

'It definitely is something to be aware of but, hopefully going forwards, it will start to get better,' said Brian.

After the meeting, Brian and I arranged to meet at the hospital that afternoon to tell Louisa about starting the visits to my house.

'I'm quite nervous about it as I don't know how she's going to react,' I told him.

'It will be fine,' he reassured me. 'We're giving her plenty of notice so it will give her time to process it and get used to the idea.'

It would just be a short visit at first and we would build it up from there.

I was already at the hospital when Brian arrived. I got us both a cup of coffee and we sat around Louisa's bed.

Now she was stronger, the staff were helping her to get dressed into her own clothes rather than her being in bed all day. They were doing everything they could to prepare her for normal life outside of the hospital.

'Louisa, I've been hearing about how well you're doing,' Brian told her. 'I know you've been working really hard with your physio and your speech therapy and you're doing amazingly.'

Louisa shrugged.

'You're doing so brilliantly that the hospital's going to start looking at discharging you, which is great news.'

'What, I can leave?' asked Louisa, looking shocked.

'Yes,' nodded Brian. 'You'll continue your rehab outside of the hospital and have to come back for check-ups, but you've recovered so well that they don't think you need ongoing medical care.'

'But where will I go?' she asked.

Nerves fluttered in my stomach.

'As we've always talked about, you will go to Maggie's house and continue your rehab there.'

'But I don't want to go to her house,' scowled Louisa. 'I want to go to my house.'

'Don't worry,' said Brian cheerfully. 'We're going to start organising some visits so you can spend some time at Maggie's house and see where you're going to be living.'

'I've got all of your stuff from your old bedroom there,' I told her. 'So you can unpack your things and put them where you want to and make it your own.'

'But I don't want to go,' Louisa muttered. 'I want to go back to my house.'

'Louisa, your mum and dad have died. The house you had was rented and it's had to go back to the people that own it so it can be rented to someone else,' Brian told her.

But she closed her eyes and I could see that she was still refusing to accept it.

*

A few days before Louisa's first visit to my house, an occupational therapist called Melodie came round to do an assessment of the house to help make it more accessible for Louisa when she came to live here. She would also be the person bringing Louisa from the hospital in an accessible taxi when she came to visit.

Melodie was an enthusiastic, smiley woman in her late twenties whom I knew Louisa would like.

'The long-term aim is for Louisa to be pretty much fully mobile by the time she's discharged from hospital,' I explained. 'So ideally she would be able to manage the stairs and only use the wheelchair when she went out.'

Melodie measured the front door and thankfully it was wide enough for a wheelchair to get through. As were the doors to the rooms off the hallway. I also had a downstairs toilet that Louisa could use when she visited.

'Long-term, there are a few adaptations that would need to be made,' she told me.

They included a handrail next to the bath, a seat in the bath and an extra handrail on the stairs. That all needed to be sorted out before Louisa came back to live with me.

Louisa's first visit was organised for the following week. We were going to keep it short – just half an hour – as I knew it would be exhausting for her. I was nervous about it as I still wasn't sure how things were going to go.

'She'll be fine once she gets there,' Brian reassured me.

He was going to pop in and say hello.

When the time came, everywhere was sparkling clean and I brightened the kitchen up with a big bunch of tulips and daffodils. As Louisa wouldn't be going upstairs on this visit, I brought down a few boxes of her clothes so she could sort through them and perhaps take a few things back to the hospital with her.

Just after 10 a.m. I saw the accessible taxi pull up outside and I rushed to the front door to greet them.

Melodie was wheeling Louisa down the ramp.

'Hi,' I smiled. 'Come on in.'

Despite Louisa's glum face, I was trying to be as cheerful and welcoming as possible. As Melodie pushed her into the hallway, I could see there was part of her that was curious about where I lived.

'This is a lot bigger and nicer than I thought,' she said, looking around.

'Oh I'm glad,' I smiled.

Melodie wheeled her through to the kitchen and I got us all a drink and a biscuit.

'By the time you visit again, hopefully you'll be able to manage the stairs so I can show you your bedroom,' I told her. 'In the meantime, I've brought some of your stuff down so you can have a look at it and sort through it. There might be some clothes you want to take back with you to the hospital.'

I hoped that it would help make it more real for her. Now she'd been to the house and seen her things here, perhaps she'd accept that this was going to be her home.

As she was looking through the boxes, there was a knock at the door.

'That will be Brian,' I told her. 'He said he was going to pop round and say hello.'

I went to let him in.

'How's it going?' he asked quietly.

'So far, so good,' I shrugged.

While Brian had a chat to Melodie about the adaptations that needed to be made, I showed Louisa the front room and wheeled her out to the garden.

'It's a lovely house isn't it, Louisa?' Brian smiled when we came back in again.

'It's bigger than my house but I don't like it and I'm not going to live here,' she told him firmly. 'I want to go back to my house. That's my real home.'

Brian and I looked at each other. We were struggling to get her to understand that her house didn't exist any more and that going back there wasn't an option.

While Melodie took Louisa to the toilet, Brian and I had a chat about it.

'Don't take it personally, Maggie,' he reassured me. 'I don't think this is about you. It's about her accepting that her parents, and the life that she used to have, have gone.'

'I know,' I sighed. 'I'm so sad for her but how do we do that? The last thing she remembers is leaving that house. She hasn't had any closure.'

Somehow we needed to give her that closure and show her that her family home as she knew it didn't exist any more.

'OK Maggie, what do you suggest?'

'I think we just have to be really logical about this,' I said. 'Perhaps we need take her to her old house and prove to her that someone else lives there now?'

Sometimes you had to give a child the reality and with Louisa's brain injury, we had to be very literal and straightforward with her. We needed to make this real for her and prove to her that her old house had gone and she couldn't live there any more.

'If you think it would help then I'm willing to give it a try,' Brian told me.

'It might upset her,' I said, 'but I think she needs to know the truth.'

Brian would drive to Louisa's old house while Louisa, Melodie and I would follow in the taxi. Afterwards, while they headed back to the hospital, Brian would drive me home.

I told Melodie the plan and Louisa didn't question why I was going to be in the taxi with her.

I knew that it could backfire spectacularly and there was a risk Louisa might not even remember her old house. But as we turned into her old street, she gasped.

'I know this place!' she shouted. 'This is my house!'

We pulled up on the street outside the row of houses.

'That's my old bedroom upstairs at the front,' she grinned. 'And Mum and Dad's was round the back.'

Suddenly her smile disappeared.

'Oh, there are different curtains at the window downstairs,' she said. 'And a baby toy on the windowsill.'

As we were sitting there, the front door opened and a blonde woman came out pushing a toddler in a buggy. Louisa looked shocked.

'Who are they?' she asked. 'And why are they in my house?'

'Louisa, remember what we said?' I told her gently. 'Because your mum and dad have died, there was no one to pay the rent on your house any more so it's been rented out to another family. They live there now. Your Uncle Martin cleared all of your stuff out of there so you've got lots of photographs of your parents and all of your things from your bedroom.'

I could see from her face that the realisation had suddenly hit. Her home, her family, was no more.

Louisa burst into tears and curled up in a ball in her wheelchair.

FOURTEEN

Blood and Tears

I wheeled Louisa down through the warren-like corridors of the hospital. Now she was able to stand, her daily physio sessions were going to take place in a therapy room rather than by her bed on the ward.

'Wow, look at this place,' I said, as I pushed open the door.

It was a huge room with all sorts of equipment in it, from crash mats and exercise balls to a small flight of steps and a walking track with two handrails on either side of it.

'Hi Louisa,' smiled Julie. 'As you can see, there's lots here to keep you busy, but today we're going to try having a go at walking.'

Helen showed her the walking track.

'There are handrails on either side so you've got lots of support,' she told her.

'But what if I fall?' asked Louisa anxiously.

'I'll walk in front of you and Julie will be behind you so if you're a little bit unsteady you've got someone to catch you. We're going to take it nice and slowly so let's aim for a couple of steps at first,' said Helen. 'Let's get you up on your feet.'

I wheeled Louisa over.

'I'll just sit quietly in the corner,' I told them.

I wanted to be there for moral support but didn't want to interfere.

Helen brought over the standing frame. But when she went to hoist Louisa out of her chair, Louisa pushed Helen away.

'No, I don't want to do this!' she shouted.

Then she turned to me.

'Don't watch me, just go away.'

She sat in her wheelchair with her arms folded.

'At least try and stand up with the support of the handrails,' Helen told her. 'You don't have to take any steps at all if you don't want to.'

'No,' said Louisa firmly. 'I told you, I don't want to do it!'

What happened over the next half an hour is what would best be described as a stand-off. Louisa sat in her wheelchair with her arms folded and refused to do anything.

'Your session is an hour long,' Helen told her. 'Julie and I have some paperwork to do so we're going to sit over there. When you're ready to try, let us know.'

But Louisa was stubborn. She sat there for the entire hour, refusing to engage with anyone. True to their word, Helen and Julie did their paperwork at a desk in the corner while I passed the time by reading some information on a training course I was doing in a few months' time.

At the end of the session, Julie went over to Louisa.

'We'll see you at the same time tomorrow and hopefully you'll feel like trying then,' she told her firmly.

I wheeled Louisa back to the ward and she didn't say a word.

'Louisa, I know this is all really hard for you but you're not helping yourself by refusing to do your physio,' I told her. 'It's you who's going to miss out in the long run. You need to be able to get up and down the stairs in order to get out of hospital and come back to my house.'

'But I don't want to go to your house,' she told me. 'I don't know you. I don't even know why you bother visiting me all the time.'

I took a deep breath.

'Louisa, when your mum and dad died, Social Services had to find you a foster home,' I explained. 'It's my home that they found and I agreed to be your foster carer.'

'I don't even know what that means,' she sighed.

'It means that I will look after you because there is nobody else to take responsibility for you. Shall I get Brian to come and talk to you?' I asked her.

'There's no point,' she replied. 'He's just going to say the same thing.'

Whenever she had these outbursts, I didn't know whether it was Louisa or the brain injury talking. I also didn't know whether it was something she didn't like about me in particular or whether it was just the idea of leaving the hospital that was scary. This hospital was her safety net and all that she had known for over six months, so I understood the idea of being discharged might well feel overwhelming. Sometimes it was important for a child just to move forwards, even if they weren't happy about it at first.

For the first time ever, I cut my visit short that day as Louisa was refusing to engage with me.

153

Unfortunately things didn't improve.

The following day, as I walked down the ward, Hannah, one of the nurses, pulled me to one side.

'I just wanted to let you know that we had a bit of an incident with Louisa earlier,' she told me.

'What happened?' I asked, concerned.

'I was taking her blood pressure and she pulled the tourniquet off, threw it onto the floor and as I was picking it up, she kicked me.'

'Kicked you?' I gasped. 'That's horrible. I'm so sorry.'

'It's OK,' she sighed. 'It didn't really hurt, it was the shock more than anything. I thought I'd better let you know.'

I'd never challenged Louisa on her behaviour before but this time, I felt like I had to. Yes, she had been through so much and I knew perhaps that she didn't have control over all her actions, but I had to pull her up on it.

When I drew back the curtain around her bed, she was sitting in a chair, staring into space.

'Louisa, I've just spoken to Hannah,' I said. 'And she told me what happened. We don't kick people.'

'I don't know what happened,' she told me meekly. 'I feel so angry sometimes.'

'I can understand that,' I replied. 'I would be angry if I'd lost my parents, and I know the injury to your brain makes you angry too. But it's not the nurses' fault. No matter how cross you are, no matter how angry you are, you don't do that,' I continued. 'You can hit the pillow or you can scream but you do not lash out at the people who are trying their best to look after you. It's not OK.'

It was the first time that I'd pulled her up on anything and Louisa looked shocked.

As the days passed, she was still being uncooperative in her rehab sessions.

I called Anna for some moral support

'We've had a week of what I can only describe as hellish behaviour,' I told her. 'Louisa's made such good progress but she's refused to do anything at all this week. She won't even try to do any of her rehab. She's rude and angry – she even kicked a poor nurse. Honestly Anna, I do feel sorry for her, I really do, but I'm starting to question my decision to take her on.'

Were her moods always going to be this much of a rollercoaster? Was this really what I wanted my life to be like for the foreseeable future? Of course, after everything she'd been through, I desperately wanted to help Louisa, I knew she had no one, but I couldn't do it if it was to the detriment of my own mental health.

'Are you saying that you want to pull out of the placement, Maggie?' Anna asked me.

'I just don't know if I can do this any more,' I sighed. 'I don't think she even likes me, never mind wants to come and live with me.'

'Maggie, take a breath,' she replied calmly. 'I can see why you're upset but I think you need to get Louisa back to your house. At the moment, you're not really fostering her – you're working around the professionals at the hospital. You need to get her home and then see how you both get on.'

Anna thought her behaviour was a reaction to everything that was going on around her.

'There's a lot of change about to happen – she'll be leaving hospital and going to live at your house – so she probably feels out of control,' she told me. 'Plus I think she's finally understood that her parents aren't around any more. Her home and her life as she knew it has gone. It's great that she's aware now but everything that has happened to her is hitting home.'

I knew that she was right.

'Yes, perhaps I just need to get her home to me and see how she gets on,' I said.

'I think so,' agreed Anna. 'Don't make any big decisions now.'

I still had a sinking feeling in my stomach as I drove up to the hospital later that morning. After the past few days, I'd come to dread my visits and what sort of mood Louisa would be in. But when I got there, she wasn't in her bed.

'She's in the rehab room,' a nurse told me.

I went down there expecting to find another stand-off between her and Helen and Julie. But, as I peered through the glass panel in the door, much to my surprise I could see Louisa standing at the end of the walking track.

I didn't want to go in and potentially disturb what was going on so I just stood there and watched. I could see that Helen and Julie were giving her words of encouragement as she stood, supported by the two handrails.

'You can do this, Louisa,' I heard Helen say. 'You've come so far. You're so strong.'

I held my breath.

You can do this, Louisa.

I could see the sheer determination and concentration on Louisa's face as, slowly and shakily, she put one foot in front of the other.

She'd done it! She'd taken a step.

'Amazing!' smiled Helen, who was behind her. 'Do you think you can try another one?'

She shook her head.

'Are you sure?' asked Helen. 'I reckon you can do one more. I'm right behind you if you can't.'

I could see it was taking every ounce of energy that she had, but she managed to take one more shaky step before Julie brought the wheelchair to her and she collapsed into it, exhausted.

I pushed open the door.

'I did it, Maggie,' she told me breathlessly. 'I walked!'

'I know you did,' I grinned. 'I was outside the door watching. That was amazing. You did so well.'

'She did brilliantly,' nodded Helen.

Over the days that followed, it was like Louisa was a different person. During each rehab session, she made further progress.

By the end of the week, she could take several steps using the walking frame or by holding onto the handrails.

'You are doing so well,' Julie told her. 'We're so proud of you. I think we'll try you on some steps next week.'

'Steps?' asked Louisa, looking alarmed.

Helen showed her the small flight of steps that they'd got. There were three steps up to a small platform and then three steps down the other side. There was a handrail on both sides to help stabilise her.

'Once you've mastered those then we can try some of the stairs in the hospital,' Julie told her.

I knew it was a really tough slog for her having to relearn everything again but it was a huge relief to see her making such positive progress.

There was a whole team of people helping to get her ready to be discharged and live in the outside world again. She had

Helen and Julie doing her daily rehab sessions, she had sessions with a speech and language therapist and an occupational therapist who was helping her to learn simple things again like using the toilet and eating with a knife and fork, things that most of us take for granted every day but for Louisa, it signalled amazing progress.

I was keeping Brian regularly updated and a couple of weeks later, we were having a chat.

'She's doing brilliantly,' I told him. 'She's confident walking with the frame now and she can do steps using a handrail to support her.'

'Now she's more mobile, I think it would be useful for her to have another visit to your house,' he told me. 'If she doesn't need the wheelchair then you could take her yourself rather than an OT having to take her in a taxi. What do you think?'

'I think that's a great idea,' I said.

I knew it would be good for us to spend time together on our own. Now Louisa could navigate stairs, it meant that I could finally show her her bedroom, which would hopefully help her to feel more settled.

'I'm going to take you back to my house for a couple of hours tomorrow,' I told her when I went to visit the following day. 'And now you can get up the stairs, we don't need Melodie to come and collect you so I can take you myself.'

'What's the point?' sighed Louisa. 'Why do I have to go to your house?'

'Because hopefully you will be coming to live with me very soon and this time I can take you upstairs and show you your bedroom,' I smiled. 'What do you think?'

'I suppose so,' she shrugged.

The following day, I wheeled Louisa out of the hospital to the car park. Once I'd helped her into my car, I took the wheelchair back to the hospital.

At my house, she used her walking frame to slowly and steadily make her way up the path to my front door. I could see that had already tired her out so I made sure we had a drink and a rest in the kitchen before we attempted the stairs.

Even though there were now handrails on both sides, my stairs were very narrow and I was nervous about Louisa tackling them. I could see she was too.

Coming down, they were very steep so I'd already decided that, for the time being, I'd show her how to shuffle down them on her bottom as it was safer.

'Take your time,' I told her. 'There's absolutely no rush. I'll be right behind you so you don't need to worry.'

'What if I fall?' she whimpered.

'You won't,' I reassured her. 'I'm holding onto the handrails so if you need to stop and have a rest, you can lean back against me.'

Carefully, Louisa managed the first three or four steps.

'Let's have a little rest,' I said.

She took a few deep breaths.

'Ready?' I said. 'Let's try the next few.'

When we got halfway up, we stopped again. I could see Louisa looking at the photographs that I'd got on the walls going up the stairs.

'Who are they?' she asked.

'They're some of the children that I've fostered over the years,' I told her.

'Oh, you've looked after other children?' she asked, surprised.

'Yes, that's what I do,' I smiled. 'I've had children coming in and out of my house for many years.'

'But where have they all gone?' she asked.

'Sometimes they live with me until they find a family that wants to adopt them or sometimes they live with me while their parents are poorly in hospital and then they go back home.'

I could see Louisa was listening and taking it all in.

'What's going to happen to me?' she asked meekly. 'Will I get adopted?'

I knew I had to be careful how I answered this as at this moment in time, we didn't know what the future held. There was no long-term plan at this stage. The plan was for her to come to my house at first and see how it went. It was unlikely that a child of Louisa's age would be adopted; the most likely alternative if things didn't work out with me was for her to go into some sort of residential care.

'You're going to come and live here with me,' I told her. 'And each day you're going to get better and better and hopefully you can go back to school again and see all your friends.'

She nodded and thankfully seemed to accept that.

Finally we made it upstairs. I could see Louisa was absolutely shattered.

'Let me show you your bedroom and we can get you sat down on the bed,' I told her.

I'd already brought her walker up so it was there on the landing at the top of the stairs.

'This is your bedroom,' I told her. 'It's a really lovely room and it gets lots of light from the big window.'

I kept it very neutral so it would suit a child of any age or gender; I would then add things depending on what they liked. There was a desk that doubled up as a dressing table and a single bed, a bookcase and a fitted wardrobe as well as the bunk beds.

'It's bigger than my bedroom at my house,' Louisa said.

'It's a bit of a blank canvas at the moment but I thought you'd want to choose where your stuff went yourself,' I told her.

All of her things were still in the cardboard boxes from when I'd packed them up at her house.

'We don't have to do it today if you don't feel up to it, but I can help you unpack if you want.'

Louisa was curious about what was in the boxes so I opened a couple of them up for her.

Her memory could sometimes still be hit and miss so I wasn't sure if she would remember her belongings but her face lit up as she looked through what was in the first box.

'Oh I remember this!' she smiled as I showed her the pinboard covered in photos that she used to have on her bedroom wall.

'Do you recognise these people?' I asked her, pointing to a photo of her with Frankie, Becky and Phoenix.

Louisa nodded.

'They're my friends,' she told me.

'That's right,' I replied. 'Frankie, Becky and Phoenix. Frankie came to see you at the hospital when you were first in there,' I told her.

'Oh,' she sighed. 'Why hasn't she come again?'

'Well, you were still very poorly then so you didn't recognise her. It was early days and your brain was still very muddled and trying to heal.'

'But it's a lot better now, isn't it?' she said.

'It is,' I smiled. 'You're so brave, you've come such a long way.'

'Do you think Frankie might want to come and visit me again?' she asked.

'We can definitely ask her,' I smiled. 'And perhaps Becky and Phoenix might want to come too.'

She nodded.

While Louisa continued to look through the box, I suddenly remembered something.

'There's something else that I want to show you,' I told her.

I quickly went down the landing to my bedroom and took out a cardboard box from a drawer.

'I got this for you,' I told her, handing it to her.

Curious, Louisa opened it up and looked inside.

'Oh,' she said. 'Teddy bears.'

She pulled out the two patchwork bears that were wrapped in tissue paper.

'Can you see anything familiar about them?' I asked her.

She looked puzzled as she put them in her lap and studied them.

'I think my mum had some pyjamas with lemons on like that,' she said, pointing to one of the patches of material.

'Yes,' I said. 'Do you recognise anything else?'

Then, after a few moments, suddenly her face changed.

'Oh,' she gasped. 'Is that really from my mum's pyjamas?'

I nodded.

'And that's her dress,' she gasped.

'And that piece is from her jeans,' I told her, pointing to one of the patches. 'Each patch of material on the bear is made from your mum's clothes,' I told her.

'Have a look at the other one,' I added.

Louisa picked it up and smiled.

'Oh that's Dad's shirt,' she said. 'And his funny jumper that he used to wear at Christmas!'

'I had them specially made from some of their clothes as a keepsake for you,' I told her. 'You'll have part of them with you forever.'

Louisa stared at them and traced her fingers over the fabric in each of the patches.

'You must miss them a lot,' I said gently. 'I've put up some pictures as well.'

I showed her the framed photos of her and her parents that I'd got from her house and put on the bedside table.

'It's good to talk about people who have died and to remember them,' I told her.

Louisa looked at me, her eyes filled with tears.

She turned around and suddenly, before I could stop her, she raised her hand and swiped the photos off the table. A picture of her parents on their wedding day hit the side and the glass on the front of it smashed.

Louisa lowered herself off the bed and sank to the floor, desperately trying to pick up the bits of glass off the carpet.

'It's OK,' I told her, firmly but gently. 'Let me do it.'

I quickly picked up the larger pieces of glass and put them out of her reach on the dressing table.

'It's not fair,' she howled. 'It's not fair.'

'I know it's not, sweetheart,' I soothed. 'It's really not fair.'

She was sobbing hysterically now. I tried to put my arms around her but she shrugged me off.

'Go away!' she snapped. 'You don't know me. You don't care.'

As she pushed me away, I felt something wet and warm on my arm. I realised with horror that it was blood, coming from Louisa.

'Louisa!' I shouted. 'Your hand.'

She looked down in shock and there, sat in the palm of her hand, was a large shard of broken glass from the photo frame, gouged into her skin.

FIFTEEN

Freedom

Suddenly it seemed like there was blood everywhere.

'Louisa!' I shouted, my chest tightening with panic. 'What on earth are you doing?'

It was almost like she didn't know herself. She looked down in a daze to see the jagged shard of glass in her palm. She'd been squeezing it so tightly, it had cut into her skin.

I quickly took the blood-covered shard from her hand and put it on the side.

'I'm sorry,' she sobbed. 'I'm so sorry, I didn't mean to do it.'

She had a horrified expression on her face as she saw the blood seeping out of her hand.

'I'm bleeding,' she gasped. 'Am I going to die? Am I dying?'

She started to hyperventilate.

'It's going to be OK,' I reassured her. 'Let's clean you up.'

I quickly opened one of the drawers and grabbed a pair of black tights that I'd bought for Louisa. I wound them round her hand to make a makeshift tourniquet and got her to press it against the cut in her palm.

'You hold that there, lovey, and I'll run to the bathroom quickly and get a proper bandage,' I told her. 'I promise I'll only be a few seconds.'

'OK,' she whimpered.

I ran along the landing to the bathroom where I kept a first-aid kit. Back in the bedroom, I removed a sterile wipe from the wrapper, pulled off the tights that were now covered with blood and wiped it over the cut on Louisa's palm. She yelped in pain.

'It's OK,' I soothed. 'I don't think it's as bad as it looks.'

Although there had seemed to be a lot of blood, thankfully the cut didn't appear to be too deep and there didn't appear to be any glass in it.

'We just need to stop the bleeding,' I told her.

I got out a dressing and stuck it over her palm and wrapped a bandage tightly around it.

'That should do the trick for now,' I told her. 'Then we'll get the nurses to look at it when you get back to the hospital.'

I sat back down on the bed next to Louisa and took a deep breath. I knew I was shaken up by what had just happened so God knows how Louisa must be feeling.

'Are you OK?' I asked her. 'I'm sorry if I upset you with the bears and putting up the photographs. I know this must all be so hard for you.'

'I'm fine!' Louisa snapped.

'You must miss your mum and dad so much,' I added.

'I told you, I'm fine,' she said firmly, clearly not wanting to discuss it any more. 'I don't care about those stupid bears.'

She suddenly seemed so angry with everyone and everything again.

'Let me go downstairs and get you a drink of water,' I told her now she was cleaned up and seemed a little bit calmer.

In the kitchen, I quickly grabbed my mobile and phoned Anna to tell her what had happened.

'Blimey, Maggie,' she sighed. 'Is Louisa OK?'

'I think so,' I said. 'I think the bleeding's stopped now but I'll get the nurses to look at it when I take her back to the hospital, just to make sure. I think she's shocked more than anything.'

'Maggie, do you think she did it deliberately?' asked Anna. 'Was she trying to hurt herself?'

'I don't think so,' I said. 'I don't think she was thinking at all. I'd given her the memory bears and we were looking at pictures of her parents and I think she was just overcome by grief and sadness and that translated to anger.'

In a way, it was the most normal reaction that she'd shown since her parents' death.

'I think now she's recovering, she's finally starting to grieve and it's hitting her hard,' I sighed.

'Poor girl,' replied Anna. 'She's been through so much. Keep an eye on her and let me know how she is.'

In the meantime, she was going to call Brian and let him know what had happened and I would also record everything in my daily notes.

I went back upstairs with a drink of water for Louisa.

'How are you doing?' I asked her.

She still looked very pale.

'I told you I'm fine,' she sighed. 'I wish you'd stop asking me.'

'OK,' I told her. 'I'm just worried about you.'

'I'm fine,' she replied. 'Just leave me alone.'

I could see Louisa was still a bit shaken up and I didn't want her to go straight back to the hospital like that so I offered to help her sort through some more of the boxes.

I pulled a few things out like posters, cushions and books and she showed me where she wanted them to go. As I lifted out a wooden jewellery box, I saw the expression on her face change and her eyes filled with tears.

'Did your mum buy that for you?' I asked her.

Louisa quickly looked away.

'I know you must miss them both terribly but it's going to be OK,' I told her. 'I promise you.'

She looked back at me, her blue eyes filled with anger again.

'What do you know?' she told me. 'And why do you care?'

'I do care,' I replied. 'I care a lot, Louisa. I know you must be grieving and I want to try to help you.'

Louisa frowned.

'Well I don't need you or your stupid teddies,' she said, throwing the memory bears back into one of the cardboard boxes.

I didn't say anything else. She'd been through enough already today and I didn't want to push her.

Half an hour later, I drove Louisa back to the hospital. She was so exhausted, she fell asleep in the car. I was hoping that this visit to my house would help reassure me, but just when I thought we were breaking down some barriers and getting to know each other, Louisa had pushed me away again. I had to be patient and hope that, given time and space away from the hospital, she would start to open up to me and let me help her.

After I'd settled Louisa back into her bed, I went to have a word with the duty nurse and explained what had happened to her hand.

'I'll put a clean dressing on it and keep an eye on her,' she reassured me.

That afternoon, when I was back at home, Brian called.

'Anna told me what happened,' he said. 'How's Louisa?'

'She's OK,' I told him. 'There was a lot of blood but thankfully it was superficial. The nurse at the hospital dressed it and doesn't think she needs stitches but it certainly shook us both up.'

"Do you think it was deliberate?' he asked.

'I honestly don't think so,' I replied.

I explained how I'd just given her the memory bears and she was looking over some of her old things.

'I don't think she was really thinking. She was upset and overwhelmed. It was a heat of the moment thing. She just gets so angry,' I sighed.

'In a strange way, Maggie, that's a positive thing,' said Brian. 'Anger is part of grieving and at least it shows us that she understands what's happened and she's trying to process it.'

'You're right,' I replied.

But it didn't make it any easier to deal with.

A few days later, I was called up to the hospital for a meeting. Brian was there as well as Helen, one of Louisa's physios, the hospital social worker, Maria, and Louisa's consultant, Dr White.

Dr White explained that she wasn't able to stay long.

'I just wanted to be the one to deliver the good news,' she smiled. 'We believe that Louisa's at the point in her recovery where she would get more benefit from being in a home scenario than the hospital. So we feel the time has come for her to be discharged.'

'That's wonderful,' said Brian. 'Isn't it, Maggie?'

'Yes,' I nodded. 'Yes, it is.'

It really was. It was such a milestone for Louisa after nearly seven months in hospital. She'd come so far from that frail, broken, confused girl fighting for her life in intensive care. I was also relieved as it meant that I could finally do my job. Up until now, I'd felt more like a hospital visitor than a proper foster carer. But naturally there was a part of me that was nervous. Was Louisa going to cope at my house? Was I going to be able to cope with Louisa? Would we get on when it was just the two of us?

'We can start planning to move her to Maggie's full time,' nodded Brian.

Dr White had to get back to the ward, so Maria took over.

'Louisa's sufficiently mobile now so that we feel she would benefit more from being in a home setting,' she told us. 'We'd like to discharge her in the next couple of days if possible?'

'Absolutely,' nodded Brian. 'As you know, she's had a couple of visits to Maggie's and an OT has done an assessment and any adaptations have already been made.'

'She can continue her physical therapy at home,' nodded Maria. 'She'll still have regular physiotherapy sessions.'

'Louisa's going to miss you and Julie,' I said to Helen.

'Oh don't you worry, she's not going to get rid of us that easily,' Helen smiled. 'She'll still be coming back to the hospital for her physio sessions, probably twice a week at first.'

By the end of the meeting, it was confirmed that Louisa was finally being discharged.

Brian wanted to go and tell Louisa the news straight away. She was sitting in a chair doing a puzzle that the physios had given her to improve her finger dexterity.

She looked up expectantly as Brian and I walked in.

'I've got some good news for you, Louisa,' he told her. 'The doctors think you're well enough to be discharged.'

She looked confused.

'You're going home,' he smiled.

'Home?' she asked 'But you said my house had gone. We saw the new people that were living there.'

'Brian means that you're going to be coming back to live with me at my house,' I quickly explained.

'That isn't my home,' snapped Louisa.

'Well hopefully, given time, it will start to feel like your home,' I told her but she looked unconvinced.

'When do I have to go?' she asked.

'You'll be leaving in a couple of days,' Brian told her. 'Isn't that wonderful? You've been so brave and worked so hard to get better.'

But Louisa just looked incredibly scared and I could understand why. The hospital had been her security blanket for so many months, it was going to be a huge change for her.

'How are you feeling about it all?' Vicky asked me when I called into her house for a coffee on the way home.

'I'm nervous,' I sighed. 'What if she genuinely doesn't like me or we don't get on?'

'You will, Maggie,' Vicky reassured me. 'You just need the time and the space to get to know each other.'

I hoped she was right. For the past few months I had felt

like a spare part and at least now I could actually get on with caring for Louisa.

I spent the next couple of days getting the house ready. To be honest, there wasn't really a huge amount to do. Louisa's things from her old house were already here and we'd unpacked quite a lot of them the last time that she was here. I'd got a new frame for the photo of her parents that had been smashed. I hesitated before I put it back on the bedside table but I still thought it was important to try to talk to Louisa about her parents and for her to have memories of them. I would ask her when she came back and if she really didn't want any photos of them around, I'd put them away. I also placed the memory bears on top of her bed but reminded myself to ask her about them too.

I spoke to Brian about how to manage Louisa's anger.

'I don't know whether it's down to grief or the brain injury,' I told him. 'But I do find it very difficult to know how to help her.'

'I meant to give you these details the other day,' he replied. 'The hospital suggested we get in touch with them.'

It was a charity that helped families of people who had suffered brain injuries and I had a phone call with one of their workers after I'd finished speaking to Brian.

'Even though she's made an incredible recovery, there are times that I can't seem to get through to her,' I told the woman on the phone.

I described how sometimes she had a blank, vague look on her face, while at other times she was very angry.

'Frustration and anger are such common issues after a brain injury,' she told me.

She described how as many as a third of people suffered from irritability to aggressive outbursts and even became violent.

'Louisa's still recovering and recovery can take years after the accident,' she told me. 'Every brain injury is different so there are no definites and it's normal for people to have a change in personality.'

When she reeled off a list of symptoms that brain-injured people could be left with, from seizures to paralysis, I realised how lucky Louisa actually was.

'She's still very tired and gets the odd headache but that's pretty much it, apart from the anger,' I said.

Her physio was going well and she'd just progressed from using the walking frame to using a walking stick as her legs were getting stronger.

Talking to this woman actually made me feel a lot better about Louisa coming back to live with me.

'It sounds like she's doing brilliantly and we're here for help and support if you need it,' she said.

'It's perhaps a good thing that you didn't know Louisa before all of this,' she added. 'A lot of people's distress is caused by the fact that their loved one isn't the person they knew before their injury.'

I came off the phone feeling a lot more positive about Louisa being discharged.

By the end of the day, her room was immaculate, the house couldn't have been any cleaner and I'd baked two tins of fairy cakes for Louisa to give to the ward staff. She could hold a pen now and make a few marks although she hadn't learnt to write again yet. But I'd bought a big thank you card and signed it on her behalf.

I hadn't done anything special at my house. I was conscious of the fact that this had never been Louisa's home, so rather than putting balloons and banners up, I kept things very low key.

The following morning, I met Brian and Anna at the hospital. Anna had offered to come and help pack up Louisa's things and then take them back to my house for me so that I could concentrate on getting Louisa sorted and into my car. Brian was there for moral support.

'How are you feeling about leaving?' he asked Louisa.

She shrugged. She seemed very nervous and quiet.

Once we'd packed her things and Anna had carried them out, it was time to say goodbye. I think I'd got more attached to the staff than Louisa. Wendy and Janet, two of the nurses from the ICU, popped down before they started their shift to say goodbye to her.

'We heard you were leaving,' smiled Wendy, giving Louisa a hug.

'Thank you so much for looking after her so well for all those weeks,' I told her, giving her a hug too.

Louisa looked shell-shocked as everyone from the nurses, physios and the OTs came to say their goodbyes. I could see how overwhelming it was for her.

'Come on then, let's get you back,' I told her, being careful not to use the word 'home'.

'Let's get you out of here,' smiled Brian.

I felt an overwhelming sense of both relief and fear as I pushed Louisa through the hospital and out to the car park. For the first time since her accident almost seven months ago, she was free to start her life again.

SIXTEEN

Learning

Louisa had been back at my house for a couple of days. We were still tiptoeing around each other.

The one thing that I had noticed was just how exhausted she was. Leaving the hospital had really taken it out of her and she'd slept most of the first day.

I was trying to give her her own space but I was on tenterhooks, and followed her around the house to make sure that she was OK. Even though all the adaptations that the occupational therapist had recommended had been done, she was still very weak and I was terrified that she would trip or fall.

I could see Louisa was already tired of me constantly fussing around her. Lately she'd been using a walking stick to help her get around but back at my house she seemed so wobbly and uncertain that she'd mainly been using the walking frame. I'd shown her how to shuffle down the stairs on her bottom, which I felt was the safest option.

'Would you like to try to have a shower today?' I asked

her, the morning of her second day. 'I can help you if you're nervous about it.'

After the OT's assessment, I'd had a plastic seat fitted across the width of the bath, which meant Louisa could sit down and then use the showerhead to wash herself.

'I'm not scared,' she snapped. 'I just don't want to.'

Ever since she had come back from the hospital, she'd been very quiet and spent a lot of time in her room.

'I hope she's OK,' I said to Anna when I called her later that morning for reassurance. 'She hasn't really talked to me and she's still very irritable and snappy.'

'Maggie, she was in hospital for seven months and she lost both her parents,' Anna replied. 'It's a huge change for her, particularly after having a brain injury. After being on a busy ward for so long with people around her all the time, she's probably enjoying having some peace and quiet.'

'You're right,' I sighed. 'I should just leave her be. She's starting to process what's happened to her, I suppose.'

'That's right. Just let her know that when she wants to talk or she feels like she needs help, you're there for her,' Anna told me.

After talking to Anna, I went back upstairs to check on Louisa. She'd been in her room having a nap but when I walked in, she was on her feet with her walker.

'How are you doing?' I asked her.

'Fine,' she said. 'I'm just going to the loo.'

'Do you want a hand?' I added.

The bathroom upstairs was harder to navigate than the downstairs toilet as there was a slight step up into it and there was only room for one handrail next to the toilet whereas the downstairs toilet had two.

'I told you I'm fine,' she said firmly.

'Well, give me a shout if you're struggling,' I told her. 'I know my toilets are a bit trickier to use than the accessible ones in the hospital.'

I had to remember what Anna and I had just talked about and let her learn to do things for herself so she felt like she had some independence. I left her to make her own way to the bathroom with her walking frame while I went to my bedroom to do some tidying.

I was putting some clothes away in a drawer when suddenly I heard a loud yelp and then a thud.

'Louisa?' I shouted.

There was no answer.

I dropped the washing I'd been putting away and ran out onto the landing.

'It's OK, Louisa,' I yelled. 'I'm coming.'

I twisted the knob on the bathroom door but it was locked.

'Give me a minute,' I said.

Although I had a lock on the door, over the years I'd had children lock themselves in the bathroom threatening to self-harm so I needed to know that I could access it at all times.

I ran to my bedroom, picked up a coin from the little pot of spare change I kept on my dressing table and raced back to the door.

'Nearly there,' I reassured her.

I twiddled the coin in the lock until eventually I heard a click.

My heart was in my mouth as I pushed open the bathroom door, unsure of what I was going to find. Louisa was lying on the tiled floor, whimpering. Her tracksuit bottoms and pants were pulled down and she was lying in a pool of what looked like her own urine.

'Go away,' she mumbled. 'Don't look at me.'

Her face burned with humiliation.

'Oh my goodness, Louisa,' I gasped. 'Are you OK? You need to let me help you.'

I got a towel and put it over her bottom half so she didn't feel so exposed and vulnerable.

'Tell me what happened,' I asked gently. 'Are you hurt?'

She turned her head away and wouldn't look at me as she spoke.

'I don't know,' she sighed. 'I was on the loo and I think I lost my balance.'

I could see she was mortified.

'Have you hurt yourself?' I asked her.

'I don't think so,' she said. 'I banged my elbow on the floor but I can move it.'

'You're probably going to have a big bruise there tomorrow,' I told her. 'Let's get you back on your feet so we can get you cleaned up.'

I tucked the towel around her waist so it made a makeshift skirt. Then I put her walker in front of her and helped to hoist her to her feet.

Slowly, I helped her back down the landing to her bedroom. We took it steadily and I could see that she was shaken up but moving okay. It reassured me that nothing was broken or bruised, except possibly her pride.

'I'm sorry,' she said wearily, as I helped to lower her down onto the bed. 'I'm so useless I can't even go to the toilet on my own. I'm like a stupid baby that wets their pants.'

I could see her eyes glistening with tears.

'You've got absolutely nothing to be sorry about,' I reassured her. 'You've just come out of coma, Louisa, it's no wonder you're still a bit wobbly. You're lucky to be alive.'

'Sometimes I don't feel very lucky,' she shrugged and I could have kicked myself for my choice of words.

'It's going to take time for you to recover,' I told her. 'You're in a new place and you don't know your way around yet. I'm here for you so don't be afraid to ask me for help, OK?'

She nodded. In a strange way, it was good to see her vulnerable side and I felt gratified that she would accept my help.

I got some clean clothes out for her. During her physio sessions, Helen and Julie had taught her how to dress herself and I'd bought her some comfy, easy-to-pull-on clothes such as tracksuit bottoms and sweatshirts.

'Do you want some help?' I asked her.

'No, I can do it,' she said. Then she paused. 'Actually, I think I would like to have a shower. Can you help me?'

I could see she was nervous after what had happened with the toilet.

'Of course I can,' I told her. 'I'll show you how it all works.'

I knew it was mortifying for a teenage girl to have to be naked in front of me. She already felt vulnerable so I didn't want to add to her humiliation.

'You can put a swimming costume on if that would make you feel more comfortable?' I suggested.

'No, it's OK,' she shrugged.

She sat on the bed and undressed herself while I went and quickly cleaned up the bathroom. Then I helped her into a dressing gown.

She'd practised using a shower at the hospital but not a bath yet and I wanted to make sure that she could safely use my bathroom.

She sat on the seat at the side of the bath and I taught her how to turn her body and lift one leg and then the other until they were both in the bath.

I showed her how to use the nozzle to wash herself while she was sitting down.

'Do you want me to help you wash your hair?' I asked her.

'Thanks, but I'll try to do it myself.'

I knew I had to let her try and regain some of her independence.

'When you're ready, pass me your dressing gown,' I told her, pulling the shower curtain around the bath. 'Then I'll leave you to it. Give me a shout when you've finished and I'll come and help you out.'

Ten minutes later, she was done.

'Does that feel better?' I asked her as I helped her back onto her feet and she nodded.

'I managed to do it myself,' she smiled.

'You did brilliantly,' I nodded.

It was great to see her building up her confidence, albeit slowly.

I kept things very simple and quiet over the next few days as Louisa got used to the house and we got used to each other. Brian dropped in one morning.

'I thought I would just pop in quickly and say hello,' he smiled. 'How are things going?'

'OK,' shrugged Louisa.

He wanted to talk to us about school.

'At this point in time, it's probably too much for you to physically go back to school so we're going to organise a tutor to come here. It will just be an hour or so at first, just to see how you get on.'

'That sounds good doesn't it, Louisa?' I said and she nodded.

She wasn't very talkative and Brian didn't stay very long.

'I'll catch up with you later, Maggie,' he told me.

A few days later, I could see that Louisa could do with a bit of cheering up. An idea had been forming in my mind and I decided to put it to her.

'Louisa, would you like to see some of your friends?' I suggested. 'I could ask Becky, Phoenix and Frankie if they wanted to come round and visit you? You know, the girls in the photographs in your bedroom,' I added, in case she was struggling to remember.

'I know who they are,' she snapped. 'I'm not stupid.'

She thought about it for a minute.

'Yes, OK,' she nodded.

I'd already spoken to Frankie's mum, Margaret, about it to check the girls were willing to come before I mentioned it to Louisa. I'd explained that it would be a short visit as Louisa was still very tired.

Understandably, Margaret had her concerns.

'Frankie was very upset after the last time she went to see Louisa in the hospital,' she'd said to me.

'Louisa's come such a long way since then,' I'd reassured her. 'Both in terms of her memory and her physical ability. I think she'd really benefit from seeing the girls and spending some time with people her own age.'

We agreed that they would come round one Saturday afternoon. But, as their visit approached, Louisa seemed apprehensive.

'What will we do?' she asked.

'You can chat or watch a film or hang around in your bedroom. Whatever you like. I know how much teenagers eat so I'll get some snacks in,' I joked.

On the day itself, I could see Louisa was getting nervous.

'When they come, can we just stay downstairs?' she asked me. 'It's easier for me to get around that way.'

'Of course you can, flower,' I said. 'Your friends just want to see you – they won't care where you are.'

The girls were all getting the bus over to my house together. Louisa was waiting anxiously in the hall for them to arrive and when I opened the front door, Becky and Phoenix squealed loudly and I noticed Louisa flinch.

'Lou Lou!' Becky gasped, throwing her arms around her.

'We're so glad you're better,' smiled Phoenix.

Frankie hung back as if she wasn't sure what to do.

'Hi Louisa,' she said.

'Hello,' she smiled shyly.

'Come through to the living room, girls,' I told them.

I could feel Louisa bristle with embarrassment as her friends stared at her walking frame as she slowly made her way to the front room.

'I can walk now, you know,' she said. 'I'm not going to have this stupid thing forever.'

In the living room, she struggled when her frame got caught on the corner of the rug.

'Do you want us to help you?' asked Phoenix.

'No!' snapped Louisa. 'I can do it myself.'

I could see the girls were a bit taken aback by her rudeness.

'Help yourself to snacks,' I said, hoping to distract them with the array of biscuits, sweets and drinks I'd put out on the coffee table.

'I'll leave you to it,' I told them.

'I'll just be in the kitchen if you need me,' I added to Louisa and she nodded.

As I got on with making dinner for that night, I could hear them chatting, laughing and screeching like teenagers do. I desperately hoped Louisa was having a good time.

Ten minutes later, I popped my head round the door to check. Becky, Phoenix and Frankie were chatting loudly about school and who fancied who.

'Frankie's got a crush on Danny,' Phoenix laughed.

'You remember Danny, don't you, Louisa?' Phoenix asked her. 'The one with the gelled hair who always plays football at break?'

But Louisa didn't answer.

She was sat staring into space with a blank look on her face. It was as if she wasn't really there.

'Louisa, are you OK?' I asked her.

No answer. That blank look again.

'Louisa?'

She looked up at me with large, confused eyes.

'I want everyone to go home now,' she said matter-of-factly.

Becky, Phoenix and Frankie shifted uncomfortably in their seats, unsure of what to do.

'I said, just go home!' she shouted at them.

I could see Louisa was upset and I knew I had to take charge of the situation.

'Thanks so much for coming girls, but I think Louisa's very tired now. Can I walk you to the bus stop?'

'It's OK,' replied Phoenix. 'We're going into town now so we know where we're going. Bye Louisa,' she added cautiously.

'Yeah bye,' said Becky.

'See you soon,' said Frankie meekly.

Louisa stared into space and didn't say a word as I saw the girls to the front door.

'Louisa didn't mean to be rude but after everything she's been through, she gets very tired sometimes,' I reassured them.

'The old Louisa never got angry like that,' sighed Frankie.

'I'm sure she'll be back to her old self soon,' I told them. 'Remember she was in hospital for a long time and, even now, she's still recovering.'

Once I'd waved them off, I went back into the living room where Louisa was sat on the sofa in a daze.

'Was that all a bit too much for you, flower?' I asked gently and she nodded.

'They were all talking and I couldn't understand what they were saying and it was so loud, it hurt my ears,' she sighed.

I could see she was really distressed and agitated. Maybe it had been too much, too soon?

The only time we went out was when I took Louisa for her physio session. I could see it was almost a relief for her to be back in the confines of the hospital – it was her safe place.

She was pleased to see Helen and Julie and the two women greeted her like an old friend.

'Louisa!' smiled Helen. 'We've missed you. How are you doing?'

'OK,' she said.

Helen took her over to use some of the equipment.

Julie took me to one side. 'How's she been getting on?'

I explained how we'd had a rocky few days and that Louisa still had lots of angry outbursts.

'It's so hard with brain injuries,' she sighed. "I'm no doctor but I've worked with a lot of patients with brain injuries over the years so I know quite a lot about them.

'It can help to know the triggers,' she continued. 'So, for example, busy places can be difficult for someone with a brain injury because of the noise and the crowds and the bright lights and it can be difficult for them to process all of the information.'

I explained how she'd got angry after her friends had come round.

'Even things like watching her friends chatting could have caused her to feel sad,' she sighed. 'She probably feels very different to them after everything she's been through.'

'I think you're right,' I sighed. 'She was finding it very difficult to follow the conversation.'

I blamed myself. 'I should have thought more carefully before I suggested it,' I told her.

'Don't beat yourself up about it, Maggie,' replied Julie. 'You're both learning. Sadly people are often different after a brain injury and that's hard for them and other people around them to accept.'

I hadn't known the old Louisa so I couldn't imagine what it was like for families of other patients seeing their loved one change beyond recognition.

'Why don't you go and have a break, Maggie?' Julie told me, patting my arm. 'You look like you could do with one and Louisa will be fine with us.'

I knew Louisa felt totally comfortable with Helen and Julie so while she had her session, I could take the opportunity to pop to the shops.

'You know what, I think I will,' I told her.

I went off to a nearby supermarket to get a few bits and pieces. I made sure that I was back five minutes before Louisa's session was due to end.

As I walked down the corridor, I could see Julie waiting outside the physio room.

Suddenly I had a funny feeling.

'Is everything OK?' I asked as I walked towards her. 'What's happened?'

'Oh Maggie,' she replied. 'I just wanted to catch you before you went in to see Louisa. I need to tell you about something that happened during our session today.

'Louisa made an allegation. A serious one at that and I wanted to talk to you about it as soon as I could.'

My heart sank. I was dreading what I was about to hear as I knew it could change everything.

SEVENTEEN

Memories

So many questions were racing through my mind.

'What sort of allegation did Louisa make?' I asked, confused. 'And who was it about?'

Allegations were something that I particularly dreaded as a foster carer. If a child made an allegation against you, they would instantly be removed from your care and an investigation could take months.

I was wracking my brains but I really couldn't think of anything that I could have possibly done.

'The allegation was about her social worker,' Julie told me.

'Brian?' I asked, shocked and surprised. 'What did she say he'd done?'

Julie explained that Louisa had said that Brian had hit her.

'Hit her?' I gasped. 'When did she say that this had happened?'

'I don't know, Maggie,' she replied. 'I didn't ask for any more details. I explained that with something as serious as this, she needed to talk to you directly about it.'

I was just so confused and I couldn't understand it.

'OK,' I sighed. 'Thank you for telling me.'

I decided not to say anything to Louisa about it until we got home and I could talk to her properly. All I could hope was that Julie had somehow got the wrong end of the stick, but it seemed unlikely.

When we walked into the physio room, Louisa was chatting to Helen and she seemed in a good mood.

'Hi Maggie,' she smiled.

'Have you had a good session?' I asked her and she nodded.

'She's been brilliant,' said Helen. 'As you requested, Maggie, we've been working on how to get in and out of baths safely and on and off toilets today.'

'That's great,' I said.

I didn't say anything to Louisa until we got home. I could tell she was tired after her rehab but I knew that this couldn't wait.

'Before you have a lie down, flower, come into the kitchen and I'll make you a drink,' I told her.

She got herself settled at the kitchen table while I boiled the kettle, then I sat down next to her.

'Julie mentioned that you said something about Brian today,' I said casually.

Louisa nodded.

'Yes, I did,' she said firmly. 'I told her that he'd hit me.'

'When did that happen?' I asked her.

'The other day when he came round here to talk to us about the tutor,' she told me.

'Why on earth did he hit you?' I asked her.

She proceeded to tell me how Brian had got cross because she wasn't walking fast enough.

'I was using my walker to get across the kitchen, but he said I was too slow so he slapped me across the face,' she sighed. 'He's really mean, Maggie.'

I couldn't believe what I was hearing and every instinct was telling me that this wasn't true. As Louisa was talking, I'd already quickly gone through the events of that morning in my head. Brian had only been at my house for around fifteen minutes and I was with him and Louisa in the kitchen the entire time. I was 100 per cent sure that they had never been alone. But why would she make something like this up?

'I'm sorry to hear that, Louisa, but I didn't see Brian do that to you,' I told her. 'Where was I when this happened?'

'I think you were in the toilet,' she replied.

'And did you say anything to him?' I added.

'Yes, I told him that it had hurt so he stood back.'

'Did it leave a mark?'

'I don't think so,' she shrugged.

'Why didn't you say anything to me when I came back from the toilet or when Brian had gone?'

Louisa looked puzzled.

'I think I just forgot,' she shrugged. 'But I remembered today.'

I couldn't understand where this was coming from. She'd always seemed to like Brian and got on well with him.

'Louisa, any allegation like this against a social worker has to be taken very seriously,' I told her. 'I'll have to refer this to Social Services and they will have to do an investigation and Brian might lose his job.'

'Good,' Louisa nodded. 'Because he really hurt me and he shouldn't be allowed to slap a child.'

I knew it had to go through the proper process but it all sounded so unbelievable to me.

Brian was the most mild-mannered man. He'd been a social worker for over thirty years and it sounded so out of character. And, vitally, I knew that I'd been there the whole time.

I had one last attempt to talk to her about it before I rang it in.

'Louisa, I've been thinking about that morning when Brian was here and I'm sure I didn't go to the toilet,' I told her. 'I was here the whole time.'

'So you must have seen him hit me too,' she said.

I knew I had to report this as soon as possible.

'How are you feeling?' I asked Louisa.

'I'm quite tired now,' she sighed.

'Why don't you go and have a nap and I'll do us some lunch when you wake up?'

I knew that would give me to time to call Anna and explain to her what had happened.

When Louisa was safely upstairs, I picked up the phone to Anna and told her about the allegation that Louisa had made.

'What do you think, Maggie?' she asked me.

'Louisa seems very upset about it and I don't want to doubt her but I can't see how it could possibly be true,' I sighed. 'I've gone back over everything in my mind, – he was only here for fifteen minutes at the most and I was in the room the entire time. They were never on their own together and I didn't even go to the loo. I just can't see how it could have happened.'

'And Louisa never mentioned anything to you after he'd left?' asked Anna.

'Nothing,' I said. 'She didn't say a word and she didn't seem particularly agitated or upset. I didn't notice a red mark on her face either.

'What will happen now?' I asked.

I knew any allegation made by a child against a social worker or a foster carer had to be taken seriously.

'I'll have to call Sharon, Brian's manager at Social Services, and let her know and then they'll take it from there.'

By the time I put down the phone, I felt exhausted. I was just so confused by everything Louisa was saying and struggling to understand why she was alleging this.

Later that afternoon, my mobile rang. It was Brian.

'Maggie, my manager Sharon's just had a chat with me and told me what Louisa has said. Honestly, I don't know where this has come from. I can promise you that I've never laid a finger on Louisa. I certainly wouldn't hit any child, especially someone who has been through so much and has been so poorly. The whole thing makes me feel sick.'

'I know,' I told him. 'I'm so sorry that you're having to go through this.'

I didn't know Brian particularly well but we'd worked together for the past seven months and all I had seen was someone very professional, kind and caring who had Louisa's best interests at heart. He had shared my joy and relief when she had come out of her coma and, I knew how painful these allegations must be for him.

'What's going to happen now?' I asked him.

'I honestly don't know,' he said.

'Surely Sharon has to realise that there isn't a shred of truth in this and it would be wasting everyone's time if there was an investigation?'

'But Maggie, they have to,' he sighed. 'Why would Louisa make something like this up?'

'I honestly don't know,' I sighed. 'All I can think is it must be something triggered by her brain injury.'

'Perhaps, but how can I prove that?' he said. 'I look like I'm just coming up with excuses.'

Now it was being dealt with, I didn't mention it to Louisa again and she didn't ask about it.

The following day, Sharon called me.

'Are you positive that Brian wasn't ever alone with Louisa that morning?' she asked me.

'Absolutely positive,' I replied. 'If I had any doubts then I would tell you, but this definitely didn't happen at my house.'

'I just can't understand why Louisa is saying this,' she sighed. 'Do you think this is anything to do with her coming out of a coma?'

I said that I'd had the same thought.

'I'm actually due to have a chat with Louisa's consultant this week,' I told her. 'If it's all right with you and you don't feel like it's breaking confidentiality, I could chat to her about it and see what she thinks?'

'Yes please, Maggie,' she replied. 'I'm keen to get this sorted out.'

When I called Dr White the following day, I explained that Louisa had made an allegation.

'I obviously don't personally know the social worker involved and it's not to say the allegations aren't true,' she said, 'but I have had patients in the past who have experienced something called confabulation after a traumatic brain injury.'

'Confabulation?' I questioned. 'What's that?'

She described how, in simple terms, it meant that the patient created false memories.

'It's really difficult because the person who does this believes that what they're saying is entirely true and accurate,' she said. 'Often there's no reason for it but they do believe that it actually happened. Louisa isn't intending to deceive people but it's her brain working to fill a gap in her memory, or it could be a result of some brain damage.'

'Thank you so much,' I told her. 'You've been so helpful. Please could you send me an email explaining all of this.'

'Yes, I'll do that. If you need anything else, please give me a call or let me know,' she said. 'Life after a brain injury can be so hard to navigate, both for the patient and their carers, so I'm happy to help if you or Louisa are struggling with anything.'

'Thanks, I really appreciate that,' I said.

The email from Dr White explaining about confabulation came the next morning and I sent it on to Sharon and Anna.

A couple of days later, Brian called me. He sounded very downcast.

'Do you know what's going to happen?' I asked him.

'Well thanks to your email, my manager spoke to the consultant too and because of that and your statement, she doesn't feel there's a case to answer to or the need for an investigation.'

'That's great news,' I said. Naturally he wanted to avoid the stress of an investigation.

'But despite all of that, I don't think I can continue as Louisa's social worker,' he sighed. 'In her mind, this really happened so she's not going to trust me and feel comfortable with me ever again and I don't think I can put her through that.'

He was also worried that it could happen again and Louisa would make other allegations.

'So I've requested to my manager that I'm removed as her social worker with immediate effect,' he said.

'I'm so sorry to hear that,' I told him. 'But I understand.'

There needed to be that trust between a child and their social worker. There were times when they would have to be alone to talk about how they felt about their placement without the foster carer being around. I knew both Brian and Louisa wouldn't have felt comfortable in that situation.

'Who's going to be taking over?' I asked him.

'My colleague Belinda,' he replied. 'She's really lovely and I think you and Louisa will like her. As you know, normally if you're withdrawing from a case, the social worker would come round and say goodbye to the child, but in this case, I don't think it's a good idea. It wouldn't be fair on Louisa and I don't want to distress her.'

'I totally understand and thank you so much for all of your help,' I told him.

'I'm sorry not to be working with you any more but please keep me updated from time to time about how Louisa's getting on,' he added. 'I only want the best for her after everything she's been through.'

'I know you do,' I said. 'Hopefully our paths will cross in the future.'

He'd been with Louisa from the start and I felt really sad about how things were ending.

Belinda came round the next day to introduce herself and she couldn't have been more different to Brian. She was tall and willowy with long blonde hair almost down to her waist. She wore a long flowing skirt and lots of jewellery.

'I'm Belinda but you can call me Belle,' she told Louisa. 'I've replaced Brian as your new social worker.'

'Good,' nodded Louisa. 'He wasn't very nice.'

Belle diplomatically didn't answer and seemed very upbeat and positive.

'I've been reading your file, Louisa, and my goodness you're such a brave girl. How are you doing?'

'I'm doing OK,' Louisa nodded.

'I also noticed from the paperwork that it's your birthday next week,' she smiled. 'What have you got planned?'

I saw the surprise on Louisa's face and I'm sure it showed on mine too.

'Oh is it?' she asked. 'I didn't remember.'

I hadn't realised either and I was grateful to Belle for the reminder.

'We'll definitely do something,' I told Louisa. 'You've got to celebrate turning fourteen.'

I quickly had to come up with a plan. It felt a bit sad if it was just the two of us celebrating at home. I was desperate to try to bring a bit of fun and joy back into Louisa's life but I also knew how overwhelmed she'd felt when her friends had come round.

I rang Anna for advice.

'I could invite my friend Vicky round for a birthday tea?' I suggested.

Louisa hadn't met Vicky before but she'd heard me talking about her. She was currently fostering two sisters, Eve and

Hannah. They were placid, sweet little girls who were six and eight.

'Do you think that would be too much for her?' I asked Anna.

'It might be different with new people,' she said. 'They didn't know Louisa before all of this so there are no expectations of how she should act.'

Much to my surprise, when I ran it by Louisa, she seemed keen.

The day before her birthday, when she was at her physio session, I whizzed to the supermarket and picked up some things to make tomorrow's tea party. Louisa was eating normally now. I tried to make it look like an afternoon tea so I was going to have dainty sandwiches, some quiche and sausage rolls and I picked a cake with blue icing as I'd remembered that it was Louisa's favourite colour. I wanted to do something nice for her but keep it very relaxed and casual.

I'd chosen some toiletries and art stuff as presents. I'd deliberately steered away from anything connected to her mum and dad or that would make her emotional. I tried to mention them whenever I could but Louisa had made it clear that she didn't want to talk about them. Her grief still seemed to manifest itself in anger and frustration and I didn't want to risk that on her birthday. I wanted her to try to feel like a normal fourteen-year-old for a few hours.

The next morning, I made scrambled eggs on toast, put it on a tray and took it up to her bedroom.

'Good morning,' I smiled. 'Breakfast in bed for the birthday girl.'

'Ooh I've never had that before,' she told me.

She had a quiet morning and a lunchtime nap so she would have enough energy to get through the afternoon. Vicky and the girls arrived just after 3 p.m.

The girls ran in and said a shy 'hello' to Louisa and I introduced everyone.

'What's that?' eight-year-old Eve asked, pointing to Louisa's walking frame.

I worried that her question would upset Louisa but she just smiled.

'That's my walker,' she said. 'I got hurt in an accident so it helps me walk while I get better.'

'It's really cool,' smiled Eve.

'Yeah,' said Hannah. 'I wish I had one.'

Louisa laughed. As she chuckled away to herself, I realised that I'd never heard her laugh before and it was so wonderful to hear.

I got the arts and crafts box out to help keep them occupied. Louisa sat with the girls in the front room and patiently helped them to make some collages out of stickers while I went into the kitchen with Vicky.

'Well, this is going much better than I thought,' I smiled. 'It's so lovely to see Louisa smiling and laughing.'

'She's very good with the girls, isn't she?' said Vicky.

'Yes, she talks to them in a lovely, gentle manner – I haven't seen that side of her before.'

Five minutes later, Eve and Hannah came racing into the kitchen.

'Look what we did for Louisa to wish her a happy birthday,' they yelled.

As a smiling Louisa came into the room, I saw her walker had been transformed. It was covered in stickers and had pom-poms, glittery ribbons and sparkly crystals all over it.

'Wow Louisa,' I laughed. 'That's amazing.'

'The girls have given me a disco walker,' she smiled.

'She loves it,' smiled Hannah.

Soon it was time for the birthday tea. After everyone had finished tucking into the sandwiches and quiche, it was time for the birthday cake.

As sneakily as I could, I got the blue cake out that I'd bought from the supermarket. I lit the 'one' and 'four' candles and started to sing as I carried it over to Louisa, who was sitting at the kitchen table.

As soon as they heard me singing 'Happy Birthday', the girls and Vicky joined in too.

I carried the cake over to Louisa and put it down on the table in front of her. The smile immediately disappeared from her face.

'I hope you like it,' I said. 'I saw it in ASDA and I know blue is your favourite colour.'

'Blow out the candles!' shouted Eve.

'Make a wish!' yelled Hannah.

Louisa looked up at me and I could see she had tears in her eyes. She lifted up her hand and swiped the birthday cake off the table where it landed in a heap on the kitchen floor.

Hannah screamed.

'Oh no!' gasped Eve.

Louisa looked shell-shocked, as if she didn't really know what she'd just done.

I stood there, staring at the messy mound of cake in the middle of my kitchen floor. I didn't know what the heck had just happened.

Vicky was already down on the floor trying to rescue it.

'I don't think we can salvage it,' she said.

I wasn't sure what had triggered Louisa's reaction, but it was her birthday and I was keen not to make a big deal out of it.

'Never mind,' I said cheerily. 'I think I've got a Swiss roll in the cupboard.'

'Girls,' said Vicky. 'Why don't we go and tidy up the arts and crafts then we can come back for some Swiss roll.'

While they went into the other room, I sat down at the table next to Louisa. She looked really shaken.

'Are you OK?' I asked her and she nodded.

'I'm sorry,' she said. 'I'm really sorry.'

'It's OK,' I told her. 'Let's talk about it later.'

I was still confused about what had just happened. I cut up the Swiss roll and put it on plates and everyone tucked in. There were no candles or singing this time.

Vicky and the girls left shortly afterwards and I sat down with Louisa again.

'What on earth happened with the birthday cake?' I asked her. 'I don't understand what made you so angry.'

'My mum always makes my birthday cakes and you got that one from a shop,' she said sadly.

'Was she a good baker?' I asked and Louisa nodded.

'Really good,' she said. 'Her cakes were the best.'

She described how, when it was her birthday, she would look through her mum's cookbooks and choose a cake, then her mum would make it for her.

'Could your dad bake?' I asked and she shook her head.

'Dad would light the candles and he'd always sing "Happy Birthday" out of tune,' she said, smiling at the memory. 'He was really silly.'

'He sounds fun,' I told her, squeezing her hand.

'I didn't know all of that and I'm sorry. If I'd known you liked a home-baked cake then I would have done it for you.'

'It wouldn't be as good as my mum's,' she sighed.

'You're probably right,' I smiled. 'I'm a rubbish baker but I would have tried for you.'

I patted her hand.

'I know you must be really missing your mum and dad today.'

She nodded.

'Maybe you and I could do some baking together some time?'

'I'd like that,' Louisa smiled.

Despite all of the angry outbursts, I was starting to see flashes of who I'd been told the old Louisa was; the sweet-natured girl that her friends and teachers had told me about was still in there somewhere. I had seen it in the way she was so gentle and caring with the girls and the loving way that she spoke about her parents.

'I'm sorry for throwing it off the table,' she said. 'I don't know what happened. Sometimes I don't understand why I do things any more.'

She burst into tears and I held her.

Beneath all of that anger, I could see that there was just pure grief. It seemed as if Louisa's brain couldn't cope with the sadness and it manifested itself as anger. But at least she had started opening up to me about it.

'It's OK,' I soothed, as I hugged her tight. 'It's all going to be OK.'

And, for the first time since Louisa's accident, I truly believed that it was.

EIGHTEEN

Blown Away

As time passed, Louisa and I got into a routine. I would drop her off for her physio three times a week at the hospital and once a day she would have a two hour-session with a home tutor called Vivian.

Vivian was a lovely lady in her late fifties with a gentle manner and she seemed to have the patience of a saint.

I could see it was difficult for Louisa and she was easily distracted. In her physio sessions I knew she'd been working on how to hold a pen and she was getting more dexterity but she still struggled to concentrate.

'She's doing OK,' Vivian told me. 'She can get very frustrated but I think the knowledge is all still there. I really think that once she learns to focus, she'll catch up in no time.'

They would do their sessions at the kitchen table and one morning, I quietly padded through to make myself a quick coffee. Vivian had been marking some maths that Louisa had done.

'It was a really good effort,' she told her kindly. 'But there was one page here that you didn't do so I couldn't give you any marks for that.'

Louisa's brow furrowed.

'But that's not fair,' she yelled. 'I didn't see the questions. You're so mean.'

She picked up her exercise book and flung it onto the floor followed by all of her pencils and pens. Then she got up from the table, grabbed her walking stick and hobbled out of the room.

Vivian looked shell-shocked.

'Don't worry,' I told her. 'I'm sure she'll come back when she calms down.'

'I don't think I was too hard on her; do you?' she worried.

'You were being completely fair,' I told her. 'Louisa gets very angry and frustrated sometimes, often out of the blue.'

It was a constant problem that I kept coming up against. In fact, I'd recently emailed Louisa's consultant, Dr White, about it and she'd referred me for some sessions with a neuropsychologist called Dr Langstaff.

'Do you want me to bring Louisa to the appointment as well?' I asked her.

'I can talk to patients about how they're feeling but often they find it hard to verbalise so I think sometimes it's more useful to talk to a loved one or a carer like yourself,' she replied.

She was based at the hospital where Louisa had her physio so I went to see her when Louisa was having a session one day.

'She gets so angry and frustrated,' I told her. 'And I never know how to handle it.'

'I know it doesn't make it any easier for you but it's an entirely normal reaction for patients recovering from a traumatic brain injury,' she reassured me.

She talked me through some possible triggers and coping strategies.

'You might not always know what's making Louisa angry,' she explained, 'so you could talk to her about what she thinks triggers her.'

She suggested that if Louisa was starting to feel angry then a useful exercise was getting her to calmly count down backwards from ten and once she got to one, to take a deep breath.

'Another good strategy is to agree on a prompt or a sign with Louisa that you can use when you can see that she's getting angry. So you might blow over your shoulder so it signals to Louisa that she needs to blow her anger away and reminds her that she needs to calm down.'

I'd been open with Louisa about the appointment and I talked to Louisa that night about what Dr Langstaff had suggested.

'I like the blowing away thing,' she said. 'We could give that a try.'

'I'm willing to try anything that you think could help you,' I told her.

In order to help improve her concentration, her physios Helen and Julie had suggested that Louisa and I play some simple games. I struggled sometimes to know what to do with Louisa; she couldn't focus enough to read and she wasn't keen on watching TV because she found it too noisy and difficult to follow. So I thought some easy games might work well too.

One Saturday morning, when I knew she wasn't too tired, I got out the Connect 4.

'Do you know how to play this?' I asked her.

She looked puzzled.

'I know it but I can't remember,' she said. 'I think we had one at home.'

I reminded her of the rules and we started a game. But halfway through, she dropped one of the counters in and then sighed.

'Oh, I didn't mean to do that,' she said. 'I don't want that one to go there. I forgot what I was doing.'

Before I could stop her, she'd tried to push her hand in to get the counter out. The frame opened up and all of the counters fell out of the bottom and landed in the base with a clatter.

'Sorry,' she cried. 'I didn't mean it.'

'Don't worry,' I told her. 'It's just a game. It doesn't matter.'

'No, it's my fault,' she hissed. 'I'm so stupid.'

She lifted up her hand as if she was about to swipe the whole thing off the table.

'Louisa!' I said, suddenly remembering the strategies that Dr Langstaff had given me. I puffed my cheeks out and blew on my shoulder.

Louisa froze and stared at me.

'Are you OK, Maggie?' she asked.

I nodded and blew on my shoulder again.

'Are you sure?' she asked. 'Your cheeks are going bright red. What's wrong?'

'I'm fine,' I spluttered. 'I could see that you were getting angry so I was trying to calm you down by getting you to blow your anger away.'

'Oh,' she laughed. 'Sorry, I forgot about that. I thought you were having a heart attack.'

Even though my plan hadn't worked, at least it had had the desired effect and Louisa was calm and laughing now.

Gradually, as the weeks went by, things did start to settle.

'She's doing so well now,' Vivian, Louisa's tutor, told me. 'I think we can up it to three or even four hours a day.'

Belle, Louisa's social worker, rang me one morning. She was brimming with positivity as always.

'It sounds like Louisa's doing brilliantly with the tutoring,' she told me. 'I think if she's now managing four hours, perhaps it's time to think about her going back to school. How do you think she'd cope with that?'

'I think it would be a big challenge for her,' I sighed.

Belle, Louisa's social worker, explained that Louisa could start with shorter days, settling her in gradually.

I wasn't convinced Louisa was ready. Secondary schools were busy, noisy places and I knew how much Louisa had struggled with just seeing her friends.

'I'll come round one day and discuss the options with her,' she said.

Belle popped in the following morning. Happily, Louisa seemed to have quickly accepted Belle as her new social worker and seemed fascinated by Belle's energetic, positive nature.

'I've been talking to Vivian,' she told her. 'And she tells me that you're doing so well that we think you could potentially manage going back to school now.'

Louisa looked at me nervously.

'It will be so nice for you to see other people your own age rather than being stuck here all of the time with me,' I told her.

'What, for the whole day?' she asked.

'Not at first,' replied Belle. 'It will just be for a couple of hours in the morning and then we can see how you get on.

'There are lots of options,' she added. 'You could start later so it isn't so busy, or finish earlier. If you find it tricky to be in the playground at break time then we can organise a quiet place for you to go.

'You also need to work out whether you want to go back to your old school or whether you'd prefer to start a new school that's closer to here.'

'I can go to a new school?' Louisa asked, surprised.

'Yes, your old school is a forty-five-minute drive away but there's a good secondary school fifteen minutes' walk from here,' I told her. 'So you might find it easier.'

'Can I think about it?' she asked Belle.

'Of course,' she said. 'Talk to Maggie and she'll let me know when you've made a decision.'

I could see that it was on her mind for the rest of the day. That evening when I went to say goodnight, she started to talk to me about it.

'I know it might sound weird, but even though I know I'm "me", I don't feel like "me" now,' she said. 'I feel different to how I was before. Do you understand what I mean?'

'That's not weird at all,' I told her. 'I think you've described it beautifully. It's like there are two Louisa's – the old one and the new one.'

Louisa nodded. 'I think the new Louisa wants a fresh start so I'd like to go to a new school instead,' she said.

'I'll let Belle know and she can start making arrangements,' I told her, glad that Louisa had been able to make a decision about it quite quickly.

'And I'm sure the new Louisa will make friends just like the old Louisa did,' I smiled.

After everything that she had been through, I thought it was amazing that she had the awareness that she had changed and wasn't the same person that she was before the accident. Sometimes she had the maturity of someone beyond her years and that steely strength and determination meant I knew that she was going to be OK and could make a new life for herself.

I was also pleased as I thought her decision was the right one. The only time that she'd seen her old friends, she had struggled, and I felt a fresh start would do her good.

With her starting a new school imminently, I knew there was one thing that we needed to deal with. Louisa's glossy, dark hair was getting long and tangled now and her fringe was in her eyes. I'd been putting off a haircut because I thought it might be too much for her to cope with, as her mum, Karen, had been a hairdresser and I feared that it would be a trigger for her.

I knew I needed to bite the bullet and just talk to Louisa about it.

'Your hair's getting so long,' I said. 'Your fringe is covering your eyes. It must be driving you mad. Shall we get your hair cut?'

Louisa nodded.

'I know it might feel a bit strange for you. Did your mum used to cut your hair?'

She nodded.

'She did it at home in the kitchen, and Dad's too.'

'I know it's probably going to feel a bit strange having someone else cut it,' I said gently, 'but I could get someone to come and do it here at home or you could go to a salon?'

Louisa's eyes lit up.

'I'd like to go to a salon,' she told me. 'I've never been to one of those before.'

I had a word with my hairdresser, a young woman called Kate who worked in a salon close to my house.

'Her mum recently passed away and she used to be a hairdresser so it might be quite emotional for her,' I told her.

'Poor lass,' she sighed. 'Don't worry, you know we'll look after her.'

I booked an appointment for one afternoon after physio and I went with her. Louisa seemed excited more than anything.

She smiled as Kate shampooed her hair at the basin and gave her a quick head massage.

'That feels lovely,' she smiled. 'I've never had that done before.'

But as she sat in the chair in front of the mirror and Kate began to comb through her hair, I suddenly saw her expression change.

Kate was chatting away.

'You've got such lovely long hair, sweetheart,' she said. 'It's so straight.'

Louisa closed her eyes and I could tell all the memories of her mum were flooding back into her mind.

Tears started to stream down her face.

'Is she OK?' Kate whispered to me. 'Should I carry on?'

I nodded.

I didn't say anything. I just pulled up a chair next to her and held her hand while Kate snipped away.

'We can go home if you want if this is too much for you, lovey,' I said gently.

'No no, it's fine,' she sniffed, wiping her face with the gown she was wearing. 'I know it sounds weird but they're good tears. I'm remembering Mum and when I closed my eyes, I was imagining that I was sitting in the kitchen at home and she was singing away to the radio and cutting my hair like she always did.'

'That's what people mean when they say they're crying happy tears,' I said, giving her hand a squeeze. 'Sometimes it's good to cry happy tears and that's a lovely memory.'

Kate had cut her hair into a sleek shoulder-length bob and she showed Louisa the back in the mirror.

'I think it's lovely,' Louisa told her.

'I'm glad,' smiled Kate. 'I think you're a very brave girl.'

When I went to pay, Kate ushered me away.

'After everything that poor girl's been through, I won't take any money off you, Maggie,' she said.

People could be so kind sometimes. I knew it had been hard for Louisa but it was a relief to see her finally opening up to me. Rather than it manifesting as anger, she was talking about her grief and sharing her memories about her parents and that could only be a positive thing. Gradually, she was starting to heal.

NINETEEN

Forever

As we sat in the car, I could sense Louisa's nerves.

'It's going to be OK,' I told her, patting her hand. 'I bet you're going to love it.'

It was her first day at the new secondary school and I could see what a big deal this was for her. Even though Louisa had been keen to start afresh, I could see it was overwhelming. I knew she felt different to everyone else and even though she'd had several months of tutoring, she was worried that she wouldn't be able to keep up academically with her peers.

Belle and I had talked to her new head teacher, Mr Snow, and we'd arranged for her to ease herself in gradually to see how she coped. She was going to do mornings for the first week and then afternoons for the second with the aim of building it up to full days after that if she felt that she could manage it.

'What if people ask me why I go home at lunchtime?' she worried. 'Or they might notice I walk funny.'

MAGGIE HARTLEY

'Just say as much or as little as you want,' I told her. 'You could tell them you were in bad car accident and you had to learn how to do everything again or you could tell them that it's none of their business. It's completely up to you. You don't owe people an explanation.'

We'd also organised for her to start half an hour later than everyone else so she could avoid the rush and the noise, which I knew would really bother her. The other pupils were already in registration so the building looked calm.

'Right then, shall we go in?' I said, reaching for my handbag on the backseat. 'Mr Snow said he'd be waiting for you in reception.'

'Could I go in on my own?' Louisa asked. 'I am in secondary school so you don't need to take me.'

For months, she hadn't had the freedom a normal teen would, and, even though I would have preferred to take her in myself, I understood that she wanted to do this on her own.

'Of course,' I nodded.

I got out of the car and helped her out. Then I gave her a quick hug.

'It's going to go brilliantly,' I told her. 'I'll see you back here at 1 p.m.'

She nodded.

I swallowed the lump in my throat as I watched Louisa slowly set off up the path to the school reception. She had refused to use her crutch for school and I could see that without it, she walked with a limp as one side of her body was still weak.

Deep breaths, I told myself. She was going to be fine.

I'd already spoken to the school nurse and I'd told Louisa to go and see her if she felt dizzy or tired or needed a rest.

'She will be okay, won't she?' I asked Vicky, as I sat in her kitchen with a cup of tea half an hour later.

I thought going to see a friend would help distract me although I constantly had one eye on the clock and wondered what she was doing and how she was getting on, and I continually checked my phone to make sure no one from the school had rung.

'She'll be fine,' she reassured me. 'Look how far she's come.'

That was true. A few months ago, I'd sat by Louisa's hospital bed wondering if she would ever talk again, let alone walk. It was incredible what she had achieved.

The next few hours dragged and I was there fifteen minutes early to pick her up. Eventually, I saw a tired-looking Louisa hobbling towards me.

'How was it?' I asked her.

'It was all right,' she nodded. 'It felt weird being in another school but everyone seemed really nice.'

I was so relieved and proud of her. As the week progressed, Louisa was absolutely exhausted and she spent most afternoons resting but thankfully things seemed to be going OK.

I was knitting in the living room one evening when Louisa came in. She'd had a nap after school and it was gone 7 p.m. and she'd only just woken up.

'You must be starving,' I told her. 'I'll go and warm dinner up in a sec.'

There was a TV programme on in the background about Thailand. I wasn't really paying attention but Louisa sat down and started watching it.

At one point, the presenter went to look round a temple and she described how people were lighting candles and leaving offerings for family members who had died. The camera panned to an altar laden with fruit, flowers and candles.

Louisa suddenly turned to me.

'Did I light a candle for my mum and dad?' she asked me.

It was completely out of the blue and it took me by surprise. I put my knitting down.

'We didn't light a candle, flower, but there was a funeral for them.'

'Did I go?' she asked.

'Yes you did,' I told her. 'Do you not remember any of it?'

'I don't think so,' she shrugged.

It was the first time that she'd ever talked about her parents' death.

'It was in the very early days when you'd just come out of your coma so things are probably very muddled in your head,' I added.

I talked about how her mum and dad had been buried in the graveyard of the church.

'You weren't there for that part,' I told her. 'We didn't stay very long as it was very hard for you.'

'It was in a church?' she said. 'We didn't go to church.'

I explained how her Uncle Martin had arranged it all.

'If you wanted to, one day we could go to the church and I could show you your parents' graves,' I told her.

Louisa seemed surprised.

'I can do that?' she asked.

'Yes, of course, and then if you wanted to and the church was open, we could go in and light a candle for them.'

'OK,' she nodded.

Then she got up and left the room. It was such an unexpected conversation but I was so pleased that she was opening up more and more to me.

I knew that I would have to check with Belle that she was okay about me taking Louisa to the graveyard, but I was sure she would be fine with it if she thought it might help.

When Belle next popped in for a catch-up, I told her what Louisa had said.

'Yes, of course you can take her to the cemetery,' she told me. 'I can't even imagine what the funeral must have been like for you and her.'

'It was pretty horrendous at the time,' I sighed. 'Louisa was there but not really present if you see what I mean.'

But it felt so long ago now and I had to focus on how far Louisa had come.

The following weekend, Louisa and I drove the hour-long journey to the cemetery. In the car on the way there, she was very quiet but I didn't push her to talk. I knew she still found chatting draining and I didn't want to exhaust her just for the sake of it before we got to the church.

As we hadn't been at the burial and it was quite a big graveyard, I'd already messaged Martin in Australia and asked him roughly where the graves were. He'd described how Karen and Simon had been buried side-by-side so it was a double plot that we were looking for and there wasn't a headstone yet.

The ground was very uneven so Louisa had brought her walking stick but thankfully we didn't have to walk very far.

'This is it,' I said.

There were two mounds of earth next to each other and a small plaque on each one with Louisa's parents' names, their dates of birth and their death.

I wasn't sure how Louisa was going to react seeing her parents' grave but she just stared at the ground.

'Are they really in there?' she said.

'Yes,' I nodded.

I could see it was still hard for her to believe it.

She bent down and picked up a handful of the soil and let it seep through her hands. A few weeds had started growing on the top.

'Will you take a photo of me, Maggie?' she asked. 'I've brought a camera with me.'

It was an unusual request. I'd never been asked to take a photo of someone at a grave before.

'If I have a photo then it will help me remember that it's happened,' she told me. 'It will help me believe that it's true, that they're really gone.'

'Of course,' I said.

She handed me her digital camera and I took a photo of her standing by the grave with a solemn look on her face.

'When the ground settles, you can put a headstone on the graves with your parents' names on it and a tribute to them,' I told her. 'We could get in touch with your Uncle Martin and I'm sure he would let you help choose the words on it.'

'Will you help me decide?' she asked.

'I'd be happy to,' I nodded.

When I'd brought her to the graves, I hadn't known what to expect. I was worried that she would be overwhelmed and upset but she seemed very calm.

'How do you feel about being here?' I asked her.

'I don't know,' she shrugged. 'I know I'm supposed to feel sad but it still doesn't seem real. I feel really upset when I see things that remind me of Mum and Dad or the things we used to do together. But seeing a pile of dirt doesn't make me feel anything because I still can't believe it really happened. It's all a big muddle in my mind.'

'That's OK,' I said. 'It's a lot for you to process and it's going to take time. You don't *have* to feel anything.'

The chapel was open so I suggested that we go in and light a candle for her parents. I put a donation in the slot while Louisa carefully lit one for her mum and another for her dad and put them in the holder. She sat down on a pew and closed her eyes.

'Bye Mummy,' she said out loud. 'Bye Daddy. I love you.'

Then she stood up and blew the candles out as if they were on a birthday cake. I didn't have the heart to tell her that the idea was to leave them burning in memory of your loved ones.

As we drove home, I was amazed at how open Louisa had been about her feelings. Cars were always good places to chat to children as you didn't have the pressure of eye-to-eye contact, so I decided it was a good time to ask the question that I'd been wondering for months.

'Do you remember what happened the morning of the crash?' I asked Louisa.

She shrugged.

'I remember having breakfast and Mum was going mad saying we were going to be late,' she said. 'She was blaming Dad because he took ages in the shower.'

I smiled.

'Then I remember getting to the breeders and collecting Luna,' she continued. 'We were all so pleased to see her. We put her in a crate on the back seat next to me and I was stroking her and making sure that she wasn't scared. The radio was on and we were all really happy. We couldn't wait to get her home . . .'

I heard the quiver in her voice.

'Then I don't remember anything after that,' she said in a small voice.

In a way, it was relief to know that she didn't remember the horror that had happened after that moment.

'It's lovely that your last memory of your parents is a happy one,' I told her. 'You know we can go back to the grave whenever you like,' I added.

She shrugged.

'It feels weird. It's not like they're really there.'

'You might change your mind,' I told her.

Louisa had been living at my house for over three months and there was another LAC review approaching.

'Now things have settled down a bit, Social Services are going to be focusing more on the long-term plan for Louisa,' Anna told me.

She'd come round for a catch-up and a chat ahead of the meeting the following week.

'What are your thoughts, Maggie?' she asked. 'How do you feel about fostering Louisa permanently?'

I paused. Permanency was a big deal and it wasn't something that I'd ever done with a child before. I'd fostered children for weeks, months and sometimes years, but circumstances had always led them to either being adopted, going back to their parents or moving on to residential care or assisted living if they were older.

'I've been thinking about it a lot,' I sighed. 'I've never fostered a child like Louisa before.'

Most children who came to me had relatives they visited or they had some form of contact with their biological parents. But Louisa was entirely alone in the world. She had no one.

'I know it's a big commitment so you're not going to make a decision lightly,' added Anna.

'It really is,' I sighed. 'And I don't even know how Louisa feels about it. I don't know whether she sees this as her long-term home.'

I would also want to make sure that even if I took on Louisa permanently, I would be able to foster other children alongside her.

It was something I would have to think about seriously over the next few days. I knew what my heart was telling me but I also had to think practically about committing to one child for at least the next four years until she was eighteen.

That weekend, Vicky was due to come round. She was looking after a seven-month-old baby called Ronnie for a few weeks while his mum was in hospital. She needed to take Eve and Hannah to the dentist so she'd asked if I could have Ronnie for an hour.

Louisa was ecstatic. As soon as Vicky came to the door, she was desperate to scoop the baby out of her arms.

'You're still a bit wobbly on your feet, lovey,' I told her. 'I don't want you to drop him so let's get you sat down and then you can hold him.'

'He's so cute,' she sighed. 'I just want to cuddle him.'

After we'd waved Vicky off, I carried a wriggly Ronnie through to the kitchen. Louisa got herself settled and I sat him on her lap.

'Hold him tight,' I told her.

She squealed with delight as he pulled her hair and climbed up to standing on her lap.

'Oh Maggie, would we be able to look after babies do you think?' she asked me. 'Please could we get some babies to foster at our house? I'd help you look after them, I promise,' she begged. 'It could be next year if it was too much for you this year?'

As she chatted away about how she would be fifteen then so she could babysit for me, I wasn't really listening. I was focused on two words.

Our house.

It was at that moment I realised that Louisa did see this house and me as her home. It was 'our house' now. She saw herself staying here and she wanted to make a life at my house and that felt lovely.

'Why are you smiling like that?' she asked me.

'Oh, I'm just impressed by how good you are with babies,' I told her.

'I think I like them as much as animals,' she smiled.

Now I knew what Louisa thought, I had to make my own mind up. Did I want it to be 'our house' permanently?

The LAC review took place a few days later at Social Services. Belle's manager, Sharon, was chairing it, and Anna and I were there along with Belle and Helen, one of the physios.

'As you know, I've only known Louisa for a few weeks but from what I've seen, she's a remarkably resilient young girl,' said Belle. 'Looking at her file, it's hard to believe what she's been through yet now she's back on her feet and going to school.'

She explained that unfortunately Lousia's head teacher, Mr Snow, wasn't able to make the meeting but she had chatted to him on the phone.

'Louisa has only been at the school for three weeks but he says that she's settled in well,' she told us.

'How do you feel that she's getting on, Maggie?' asked Sharon.

'She's very tired after school,' I shrugged. 'But I think that's to be expected. She's coping with it and she wants to go every morning, which is great.

'She's obviously missed a huge chunk of school so I think the teachers are very aware of that, especially in maths, but going forwards, they're willing to provide extra support if needed.'

Then it was Helen's turn to address the meeting.

'Louisa is doing brilliantly,' she grinned. 'We're down to two sessions a week now. Her mobility has really improved. She's using the walking stick less and less and she's almost back to full function movement-wise.

'I think when she's tired she does get weaker but hopefully that will continue to improve.'

Sharon talked about how Louisa had had a check-up with her consultant, Dr White, a few weeks ago.

'She wrote to us to say she was amazed by her progress,' she said. 'She's not had any major issues that are sometimes associated with a brain injury, like eye problems, headaches or seizures, and her scans were all fine. She doesn't need to see her for another six months.'

It was all overwhelmingly positive and I was so relieved as I was aware of how differently things could have turned out.

'We also need to address the long-term plan for Louisa going forwards,' said Sharon, turning to me.

'Maggie, how are you feeling about things?' she asked. 'Is permanency something that you would consider?'

Anna looked at me.

'It's not something I've ever done before,' I replied. 'And it does feel like a big commitment.'

I explained how I never started a placement with a particular goal in mind. I fostered a child as long as it was working for them and for me.

'I've gone through it so many times in my mind,' I continued. 'Even up until a few days ago, I wasn't sure if that was even what Louisa wanted but I feel now that it is.' I paused. 'And I feel like it's something that I want too.'

The simple fact was, I'd only known Louisa for eleven months and for much of that time, she'd been in hospital. But in that time, she'd fought for her life and gone through so much. There had been many ups and downs and I was sure there were many more to come as she got older and started to deal with the gaping hole of grief left by her parents' death. But I wanted to be the one to help her through that and be there to hold her hand. She had no one and I cared deeply about what happened to her.

'I didn't know the old Louisa but I do know the new one and I like her,' I smiled. 'I'm so proud of her. She's come through so much and she's been so strong. I think she's just incredible and I want to be her family.'

As I said it, I felt quite emotional. Anna reached over and gave my hand a squeeze.

Sharon nodded.

'Belle will talk to Louisa today as well just to check that she's on the same page,' she nodded. 'But I'm sure she is, and, as far as I can see, going forwards we're all happy for her to stay with Maggie permanently.

'And as you're approved to take on three placements in total, when you decide the time is right, you can take on other children.'

'Thank you,' I said. 'I think Louisa would like that too.'

Belle was keen to talk to Louisa about it as soon as she could.

'I'm due to pick her up from school after this meeting so you could meet us at home when we get back?' I suggested.

I didn't tell Louisa that she was coming because she would want to know what it was about. When there was a knock at the door, she looked at me expectantly.

'That will probably be Belle,' I told her.

I got us all a drink and we sat in the kitchen with an anxious-looking Louisa.

'How's school?' asked Belle.

'Fine,' said Louisa warily. 'Is that what you've come to talk to me about?'

'Actually we had a meeting today at Social Services so Belle wanted to chat to you about that,' I told her.

'Louisa, there's something we need to talk to you about . . ..' began Belle.

'It's OK,' she said sadly. 'I already know what you're going to say. When do I have to go?'

'Go?' asked Belle. 'Go where?'

'When do I have to move to the children's home?' sighed Louisa.

Belle and I looked at each other, bewildered.

'Louisa lovey, you don't have to go to a children's home,' I told her.

'I don't?' she asked, puzzled.

'Now I'm better, I thought I would have to go. I thought that's what you were going to tell me and that was what the meeting was about.'

'Louisa,' I said. 'You're not going anywhere.'

'Really?' she gasped. 'I can stay here with you?'

'If you want to,' Belle nodded.

'How long can I stay for?' she asked.

'Well, forever,' I laughed. 'I mean, as long as you want to.'

Louisa looked stunned.

'But you showed me all the photos of the children on the stairs and you said they had all moved on,' she told me.

'Well they had,' I replied. 'But that doesn't mean that you have to. Louisa, I would really like you to stay here with me,' I told her. 'I know I will never ever replace your parents and I don't want to, but I'd like this to be your home. What do you think?'

Louisa paused, then burst into tears.

'Oh flower,' I gasped, putting my arms around her. 'I didn't mean to make you cry. It doesn't matter if this isn't what you want,' I told her. 'I won't be offended.'

'Absolutely,' nodded Belle. 'Our priority is you and where you think you'd be happiest.'

'No, no, I want to stay here with you, Maggie. I swear these are happy tears!'

I sighed with relief as I put my arms around her and gave her a hug.

'You've been through so much and I'm so, so proud of you,' I told her. 'There are going to be hard times and times that we get on each other's nerves but we'll get through it – together. OK?'

Louisa nodded and wiped away her tears.

By the time Belle left, we were both exhausted.

That evening I made Louisa's favourite tea – lasagne, salad and garlic bread. We even had a glass of cola and a slice of cheesecake for pudding.

'I've got a present for you,' I told her. 'It's something I've been meaning to give you for a while.'

I got up and went over to the kitchen drawer where I brought out a small blue box.

'Here you go,' I told her, passing it to her. 'I've had these for a long time but I wanted to wait until I felt you were recovered and emotionally able to cope with them.'

Curiously, Louisa opened the box.

Inside was a gold chain and on it were three rings – two gold bands and a diamond solitaire.

'Oh, it's Mum's ring!' she gasped when she saw the diamond.

'And your mum and dad's wedding rings,' I told her.

'I remember,' she said, rubbing her finger over the metal.

'I wanted to find a special chain for you to put them on,' I told her. 'So you have the rings from your mum and dad and the chain is from me.'

'Can I put it on?' she asked.

'Yes, of course,' I said.

I carefully undid the clasp and then placed it around her neck. Louisa went over to the mirror.

'It looks lovely,' she smiled. 'Thank you.'

I was so pleased that she liked it.

'Even though you're going to be living with me, they will always be your parents and they'll always be with you,' I told her.

I hoped the necklace would be a reminder of the past but also give her a sense of moving forward together with me. Louisa had been through the most horrendous experience; nothing was ever going to change that or take it away. I wasn't going to kid myself that this was a perfect, happy ending – there were going to be so many ups and downs as the years passed. I knew that. But Louisa and I would get through it, together. I could offer her a comfortable home and surround her with love, and hopefully, that would be enough.

Epilogue

As the months and years passed, Louisa continued to make an astonishing recovery from her accident. So much so that now the only sign of what she's been through is an occasional headache when she gets tired.

Because of how much school she had missed, academically she never quite reached the same level that she had before the crash. But as she lived with me and spent time with all the children that I fostered over the years, she grew to have a real love for children. In fact, she was a natural with them and a great help to me in my fostering and eventually when she left school, she got a job as a nanny. A job that she still has today around her own family!

As the years passed, there were rocky times, especially during those late teenage years. There were slammed doors and lots of tears (Louisa's and mine). But all of it, both the good and bad, proved to me that taking on Louisa permanently was the best decision that I have ever made. Now, many years later, I couldn't love her more and even though we're not bound by blood, she is, and always will be, my gorgeous daughter.

Acknowledgements

Thank you to my children, Tess, Pete and Sam, who are such a big part of my fostering today – I had not met you when Louisa came into my home. To my wide circle of fostering friends – you know who you are! Your support and your laughter are valued. To my friend Andrew B for your continued encouragement and care. Thanks also to Heather Bishop, who spent many hours listening and enabled this story to be told, my literary agent Rowan Lawton and to Anna Valentine, Vicky Eribo and Beth Eynon at Seven Dials for giving me the opportunity to share these stories.

Keep up to date with

MAGGIE HARTLEY

and her heart-breaking, powerful true stories
by joining her at
www.facebook.co.uk/MaggieHartleyAuthor
for exclusive updates, first looks and special prizes.

Don't miss out on
the *Sunday Times* bestseller and Britain's
most-loved foster carer's
other stories of hope and connection...

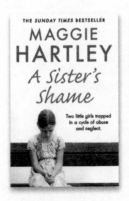

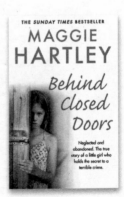

and many more,
all available now